CW00404657

The Ginologist Cook

150 Delicious Recipes with Gin.

Shane Heldsinger
Carbon Bistro

Charlotte Letlape
The Pastry Princess

Kundi Thai
Kundi's Kitchen

Phillip Tlhako
Chef

Cocktails by:

Ahe Jafta
The Mixologist

Copy Editors:

Will Campbell

Richard Prinsloo Curson

Hein Prinsloo Curson

Art Director:

Jacqués Von-Antonio du Plessis

Graphic Designer:

Thabisile Ntsele

978-1-912576-03-6 (Kindle)

A catalogue record of the printed book is available from the British Library

Gin and Tonic is the favourite alcoholic drink of Her Majesty the Queen.

It has undergone an historic journey dating back to the 13th century.

Recently we have seen a trend of craft Gins being distilled all around the world. With the wonderful flavours being infused in these spirits they have become a cook's friend, adding a brand-new dimension to classic dishes as well as inspiring new delicious cuisine.

For centuries chefs have been finding new ingenious ways to infuse alcohol with food. In earlier years alcohol was used to both preserve food and to some extent hide the taste of rancid meat.

Thankfully today we enjoy the best of cooking with booze and some famous boozy classics include Christmas pudding, crêpes suzette, beef bourgeon and steak and ale pie.

The alcohol gives a distinctive flavour to these dishes. However, many of us will not look at Gin in the same way as wine, rum or brandy when cooking.

That is set to change.

Ginologist in South Africa have been busy developing gin and working with new botanical infusions including a Floral gin which showcases the famous South African rose geranium flavours, making it possible for the first time to use this flavour in food.

Among their other discoveries and creations, the distillers have made gin a store cupboard essential and in this book have worked with some talented cooks to demonstrate just how tasty food made with gin can be.

They have been crafted, written and cooked by talented food technologists and chefs in South Africa. This book was designed in South Africa.

It is to the testament of Africa that at long last we get to see the incredible hidden talents which are embellished within this glorious, historic and beautiful continent.

Thank you Ginologist for bringing gin to the pantry and thank you South Africa for giving the world this incredible book.

BISTRO

GINOLOGIST
Carter

Contents

MAINS

DESSERTS

COCKTAILS

A brief *History* of Gin

Gin has been on a journey since it was born in the 13th Century and earned itself the name 'Dutch Courage' when English soldiers who provided support in Antwerp against the Spanish in 1585, during the Eighty Years' War drank it to steady their nerves before going to battle.

During the 17th century Dutch and Flemish distillers were re-disuntiling malt spirit or wine with juniper or coriander and these were sold as medicines for kidney ailments, stomach complaints and debilitating gout among others.

Gin had been in and out of use in England throughout the 17th century, but during the Restoration, returned as a consumable.

When William of Orange, ruler of the Dutch Republic, occupied the British throne with his wife Mary, gin was very fashionable particularly in disgusting, inferior quality solutions flavoured with turpentine!

Gin consumption in England went up after the Government made gin production legal and imposed taxes on imported spirits including French brandy.

The gin Craze happened between 1695-1735 where thousands of gin traders supplied demand across England. Because it was so affordable gin was favoured by the poor.

The Gin Act 1736 enforced taxes on sellers which resulted in riots and mayhem in the streets and was abolished in 1742. The Gin Act 1751 forced disuntilers to sell to licensed sellers.

Gin in the 18th century was produced in pot stills and was somewhat sweeter than the London gin known today.In London in the early 18th century vast quantities of gin were disuntiled legally inresidential houses (there were estimated to be 1,500 residential suntils in 1726) and was often flavoured with turpentine to generate resinous woody notes in addition to the juniper.

As late as 1913, *Webster's Dictionary* states without further comment, 'common gin is usually flavoured with turpentine'.

The invention and development of the column suntil (1826 and 1831) made the disuntilation of neutral spirits practical, enabling the creation of *London Dry* which evolved in the 19th century.

In the 1700s in India and other British tropical colonies gin was used to hide the bitter flavour of quinine, which was the only effective anti-malarial compound.

Quinine was dissolved in carbonated water to form tonic water. The resulting cocktail is 'Gin and Tonic', although modern tonic water contains only a trace of quinine as a flavouring.

Spice *Gin*

is a complex, well-balanced, pepper-lead London Dry Gin. It is a celebration of South Africa's spice palate, using black pepper, grains of paradise, coriander and so much more to create the most unique gin on the market right now. This gin's complexity lends itself well to the more ardent gin enthusiast.

Floral *Gin*

uses a dual-process approach, meaning we both vapour infuse and boil-in our flavours. The two main botanicals are orange blossom and rose geranium, both sourced locally, and both, to the surprise of many, are indigenous to South Africa. This gin is a celebration of our South African Heritage.

Citrus *Gin*

was perhaps the toughest to perfect for a number of reasons. First and foremost, we wanted to differentiate our Citrus Gin from every other gin out there. This was accomplished by using lemon, lime and grapefruit as our lead botanicals, and secondly by utilising the whole fruit, not simply the zest, to flavour the gin, to create a far smoother and well-balanced gin.

VAN LOVEREN
FAMILY VINEYARDS
VAN LOVEREN
FAMILY VINEYARDS

Starters

- Asian Coleslaw with Peanut Dressing
- Basil, Corn and Rocket Salad
- Carrot & Orange Salad
- Cauliflower & Goat Cheese Fondant
- Gin & Tonic Poached Apples
- Candied Walnuts
- Roasted Apple Purée
- Goat Cheese Crumbles
- Cheese & Pistachio Parcel
- Onion Relish
- Chicken Liver Pâté
- Chilli Citrus Oysters
- Citrus Roasted Beetroot
- Citrus Coleslaw with a Honey & Mustard Dressing
- Cranberry & Plum Sauce
- Creamy Butternut & Burnt Sage Soup
- Fig & Mango Chutney
- Flambéed Halloumi
- Goat Cheese Tart with Puff Pastry
- Tomato & Fresh Basil Soup
- Spiced Sweet Potato
- Potato & Leek Soup
- Prawn & Mussel Soup
- Puff Pastry Straws
- Vegetable Spring Rolls in Rice Paper
- Salmon Mousse
- Ginchup
- Salmon Ceviche
- Boerewors Croquettes
- Greek Salad with Soy Dressing
- Prawn & Mango Salad
- Flame-grilled Spicy Chicken Wing Skewers
- Gin & Biltong Salad
- Floral Terrine
- Cool Citrus Tzatziki
- Pork Belly Loaf
- Rose Potato Bake
- Tuna & Spice Dumplings
- Floral Tomato Soup
- Tomato Preserve
- Cheesy Bacon Mashed Potatoes
- Summer Prawn Spring Rolls

Outside at Hemingways

Asian Coleslaw with Peanut Butter Dressing
with **Fl**oral Gin

Gingredients

5 tbsp rice wine vinegar
2 tbsp *Ginologist* Floral Gin
6 tbsp vegetable oil
5 tbsp creamy peanut butter
3 tbsp soy sauce
3 tbsp brown sugar
1 tsp garlic, minced
2 tbsp fresh ginger, minced
400g mixed red and green cabbage, thinly sliced
2 carrots, grated (or julienned)
1 red bell pepper, thinly sliced
1 red apple, thinly sliced (or grated)
1 bunch fresh coriander to garnish

Ginstruction

- Place rice vinegar, gin, oil, peanut butter, soy, sugar, garlic and ginger in a medium bowl and whisk.
- In a large bowl, mix cabbage, carrots, bell pepper, and apple.
- Just before serving, pour peanut butter sauce over coleslaw and toss to combine.
- Best served immediately and consumed on the same day. Garnish with coriander.

* Serves 10-15

Basil, Corn & Rocket Salad with Homemade Gin Viniagrette

with Citrus Gin

Gingredients

4 cooked ears of sweetcorn,
(sliced off from the cob
in chunks after cooking)
Rosa/cherry tomatoes, whole
Danish feta cheese, cut into chunks
Fresh basil
Bag of rocket salad

Ginstruction

- Assemble salad starting with greens, then sweetcorn chunks, and finishing off with tomatoes and feta cheese.

For Vinaigrette

Gingredients

62,5ml *Ginologist* Citrus Gin
125ml freshly squeezed lemon juice
3 tbsp honey
185ml olive oil
Salt and pepper to taste

Ginstruction

- Vinaigrette can be made using a blender, electronic whisk, or hand whisk.
- Add gin, lemon juice, basil pesto and honey to blender if using, or bowl if whisking. Blend/whisk for a few minutes.
- While blender is on or while whisking, slowly pour in oil a little bit at a time until fully emulsified.
- Refrigerate and pour over salad just before serving.
- Keeps well in the fridge for about 3 days.

* Serves 2-4

Carrot & Orange Salad
with Citrus Gin

Gingredients

2 carrots, grated
3 oranges, chopped
1 large shot (about 45ml) *Ginologist* Citrus Gin
Mint Leaves for garnish

Ginstruction

- Place all Gingredients, including any juice of the orange lost during chopping, into a medium bowl and mix to combine.
- Chill and infuse in the refrigerator for 30 minutes to an hour.
- Serve chilled and garnish with mint leaves.

* Serves 4

Cauliflower &
Goat Cheese Fondant
with **Fl**oral Gin

Gingredients

250 grms cauliflower
250ml water
125ml milk
1 tsp cinnamon
1 tsp nutmeg
250g butter
80g caster sugar
4 eggs
4 egg yolks
100g goat cheese
6 heap tbsp self-raising flour
60ml *Ginologist* Floral Gin

Ginstruction

- Boil cauliflower in milk and water with the spices, when cooked make a purée and set aside.
- In a separate saucepan melt butter and sugar until sugar dissolves and add to the purée, mix in the eggs and flour to form batter.
- To assemble, put two tbsp of batter in the mould then slice goat cheese and put in the mould then put 2 more tbsp to cover the cheese, the bake at 200°C for 8-10min.

* Serves 2-4

Gin & Tonic Poached Apples

with Citrus Gin

Gingredients

2 Granny Smith apples
365ml G & T

Ginstruction

Peel and dice the apples, poach them in a G & T for 4 minutes.

* Serves 2

Candied Walnuts

with Citrus Gin

Gingredients

128g walnuts
64g caster sugar
20ml egg whites
Pinch of paprika

Ginstruction

Mix everything together in a bowl, transfer into a silicon mat lined tray and bake at 170°C for 10 minutes.

* Serves 2

Roasted Apple Purée
with Citrus Gin

Gingredients

3 apples
2 cinnamon sticks
4 tbsp Gin
3 tbsp butter
2 tbsp brown sugar

Ginstruction

Cut apples in quarters, add everything into cake tray, cover with foil then in the oven for 20-25 minutes at 180°C.

* Serves 2

Goat Cheese Crumbles
with Citrus Gin

Gingredients

64g cake flour
25g butter (soft)
25g goat cheese
Pinch salt
Pinch black pepper

Ginstruction

Blitz everything together in a food processor, transfer into a parchment lined tray and bake for 7-9 minutes at 180°C.

* Serves 2

Cheese & Pistachio Parcel

with **Fl**oral Gin

Gingredients

100g ricotta
100g feta
100g goat cheese
50g chopped pistachios
1 tsp chopped dill
15ml *Ginologist* Floral Gin
Filo pastry
Melted butter for brushing

Ginstruction

- Mix the cheeses together in a bowl.
- Add the chopped pistachios and mix. Add the gin and mix until combined.
- Cut the filo pastry into squares (approx: 7cm x 7cm).
- Brush with the melted butter.
- Place a tbsp of the cheese mix in the middle.
- Pull the four corners up and press together.
- Bake in an oven at 180°C for 10-12 minutes until golden brown.

* Serves 2-4

Onion Relish

with Citrus Gin

Gingredients

1kg mixed onions
(shallots, white, red, brown)
10g butter
200g brown sugar
50ml *Ginologist* Citrus Gin
20ml malt vinegar
1 tbsp olive oil
20ml brown grape vinegar
1 tbsp wholegrain mustard
2 cloves of chopped garlic

Ginstruction

- Butter the bottom of the pot (stops the onions from sticking).
- Slice the onion thinly. Add the butter and the oil to a saucepan, add the garlic and brown.
- Add the onions, and cook until soft.
- Add the vinegar, gin and the sugar and stir until sticky and the sugar has melted and it is sticky and reduced.
- Remove from the heat and once cooled place into glass jars and store in the fridge.

Chicken Liver Pâté with Spice Gin

Gingredients

250g chicken livers
1 shallot chopped
2 cloves garlic chopped
5ml mace
200g butter
25ml *Ginologist* Spice Gin
Salt and pepper to taste
10g chopped thyme and rosemary

Ginstruction

- Place 30g of the butter in a frying pan with the shallots and garlic and sweat the onions.
- Melt the remaining butter in a saucepan, and let cool.
- Add the chicken livers and cook with the salt, pepper, and chopped herbs until they are pale pink inside (don't overcook).
- Pour the gin and simmer for 30 seconds.
- Place the chicken livers and add the yellow clarified part of the butter in a food processor and blitz until smooth.
- Scoop out and place in a glass bowl and let rest in the fridge overnight.

* Serves 2-4

Chilli Citrus Oysters... With a Kick!!

with Citrus Gin

Gingredients

10 fresh oysters
1 lime, juiced and zested
2 tbsp *Ginologist* Citrus Gin
½ tsp ginger, minced
1 tsp rice vinegar
1 tsp sugar
½ a chilli, minced
(remove seeds for less heat)

Ginstruction

- Place all Gingredients, except for oysters, in a jug and whisk until combined.
- Pour over oysters and serve immediately.

* Serves 5-10

Citrus Roasted Beetroot
with Citrus Gin

Gingredients

500g fresh beetroot bulbs, cut into wedges,
with skin and stalks until on
1 garlic bulb, cloves separated and peeled
1 big bunch thyme, leaves separated
1 tsp salt
¼ tsp pepper
1½ tsp brown sugar
3 tbsp olive oil
3 tbsp *Ginologist* Citrus Gin
2 oranges, peeled, and sliced for serving
Danish feta cheese, crumbed, for serving
Pumpkin seeds, toasted and roughly chopped, for serving
Mint leaves, to garnish

Ginstruction

- Pre-heat oven at 180°C.
- Place above ingredients (except for oranges, feta, pumpkin seeds and mint leaves), in a roasting pan and toss until well-coated and combined.
- Close tightly with oven safe heavy aluminium foil and place in oven for 20 minutes.
- Remove roasting pan from oven and remove foil, then return pan to the oven uncovered, for final 20 minutes of cooking.
- Place a beetroot wedge or two on a slice of orange, sprinkle crumbed feta and pumpkin seeds, and garnish with mint leaf.

* Serves 6

Citrus Coleslaw with a Honey & Mustard Dressing

with Citrus Gin

Gingredients

150g carrots

150g cabbage

50g chopped apples

50g chopped orange segments

15g whole grain mustard

15g dijon mustard

100g mayonnaise

40g honey

30ml milk

30ml *Ginologist* Citrus Gin

Ginstruction

- Grate and julienne the carrots.
- Cut the cabbage into strips.
- Add the chopped apples and oranges.
- Whisk both the mustards, mayonnaise, honey, milk and gin until combined.
- Add the mayonnaise dressing to the carrots etc.
- Mix until combined.
- Sprinkle some crushed black pepper and serve.

* Serves 2-4

Cranberry & Plum Sauce
with Floral Gin

Gingredients

300g plums
150g dried cranberries
1 tbsp rose water
125ml water
1 tsp mixed spice
½ tsp paprika
30ml *Ginologist* Floral Gin
96g brown sugar
Zest of one large orange
1 tsbp orange juice

Ginstruction

- Combine the rosewater and gin.
- Soak the cranberries in the rosewater and gin mixture for at least one hour.
- Butter the pot to prevent sticking.
- Strain the cranberries but keep the rosewater and gin mixture.
- Place the plums, cranberries orange zest and orange juice and sugar into the saucepan.
- Add half the water and mix.
- Cook and keep stirring for 15-20 minutes until it is soft.
- Remove from the heat and stir in the gin and the rosewater.
- Place in glass jars and keep in the fridge.

Creamy Butternut & Burnt Sage Soup
with Citrus Gin

Gingredients

500g butternut
250ml cream
150ml milk
100g sage
15g butter
5g cinnamon
15g brown sugar
60ml *Ginologist* Citrus Gin

Ginstruction

- Boil the butternut until semi-soft.
- Heat some butter on a pan and sprinkle the cinnamon and sugar onto the butternut and fry (with the sage).
- Once cooked take off the heat and place into a blender with the cream and the milk and blitz until smooth.
- Place into a saucepan and heat through and the take off the heat and add the gin.
- Pour into bowls and serve.
- Note: Can be served hot or cold

* Serves 2

Fig & Mango Chutney

with Spice Gin

Gingredients

400g figs
128g brown sugar
1 tsp lime juice
400g mango (preferably stringless)
128g white sugar
1 tbsp lemon juice
50ml *Ginologist* Spice Gin

Ginstruction

- Butter 2 different saucepans.
- Peel the mangoes and place them into a pan (including the pip).
- Cover with the white sugar and place on the stove on low heat.
- Let the mangoes simmer while the sugar melts and start to stir to prevent it sticking to the bottom of the pan.
- Add the lemon juice and keep stirring.
- Place the figs into the second saucepan and cover with the brown sugar and simmer over low heat constantly stirring.
- Add the lime juice and keep stirring.
- After about 15 minutes remove the mango pips.
- Add the figs to the mango mixture and stir to combine.
- Once it is soft remove from the heat and stir in the gin.

Flambéed Halloumi
with **Fl**oral Gin

Gingredients

Fresh halloumi cheese, drained
1 large shot *Ginologist* Floral Gin
1 lemon wedge

Ginstruction

- Heat heavy bottom non-stick pan on high heat, then sear halloumi chunks for a minute or two on each side.
- Remove pan from heat and place on a safe non-cluttered surface.
- Pour shot of gin onto cooked halloumi.
- Switch on a lighter and bring the towards halloumi, quickly moving away as soon as a flame ignites (keep your head away from the pan as you ignite the flame).
- Wait for the flame to switch off, then squeeze lemon wedge over the halloumi.
- Serve immediately in a salad, alone as a snack, dipped in some sweet chilli sauce as an appetizer, or on some bread.

* Serves 2-4

Chef Shane

*"Gin uplifts the flavours and makes great tasting food **irresistable!**"*

Goat Cheese Tart with Puff Pastry &

Ginologist Floral Dressing

Gingredients

500g plain goat cheese softened
1 tbsp chopped chives
1 tbsp chopped basil
1 tbsp chopped parsley
62,5ml heavy/double cream
30ml *Ginologist* Floral Gin
Zest of 1 lemon
Salt and pepper to taste
¼ packet salty crackers biscuits finely blended in food processor

Ginstruction

Using an electric mixer beat the above Gingredients except the salty crackers crumb until smooth. Leave in the fridge to set.

For the Salad

Gingredients

100g wild rocket rinsed and drained
50g cherry tomatoes halved
60g cooked baby beetroot
20g julienne raw carrots
30g diced and de-seeded cucumber
2 large tomato de-seeded and diced
½ red onion thinly sliced
60ml extra virgin olive oil
20ml white wine vinegar
30ml *Ginologist* Floral Gin

Ginstruction

Combine all the Gingredients and set aside.

Puff Pastry

Roll out store bought puff pastry and cut a rectangular shape 10cm by 3cm. Brush with egg wash and bake at 200°C they are until golden brown and puffy. Leave to cool.

Assembly

On a flat plate spoon a tbsp of the salty crackers crumbs, using an ice cream scoop. Scoop a moderate sized ball and place on top of the crumbs. Cover the cream cheese ball with the salad mix and garnish with the puff pastry.

* Serves 4

Tomato & Fresh Basil soup

with Ginologist **Fl**oral Gin Swirl

Gingredients

15ml olive oil
25g butter
1 medium onion, finely chopped
900g ripe Italian plum tomatoes, roughly chopped
1 garlic clove roughly chopped
750ml chicken stock
120ml dry white wine
30ml sundried tomato paste
30ml shredded fresh basil
150ml double/heavy cream
50ml *Ginologist* Floral Gin
Salt and pepper to taste

Ginstruction

- Heat the oil and butter in a large saucepan until foaming.
- Add the onion and cook gently for about 5 minutes, stirring frequently, until softened but not brown.
- Stir in the chopped tomatoes and garlic, then add the stock, white wine and sundried tomato paste, with salt and pepper to taste. Bring to the boil, then lower the heat, half cover the pan and simmer gently for 20 minutes, stirring occasionally to stop the tomatoes sticking to the base of the pan.
- Process the soup with the shredded basil in a blender or food processor, then press through a sieve into a clean pan.
- Add the double/heavy cream and gin and heat through, stirring.
- Do not allow the soup to approach boiling point. Check the consistency and add more stock if necessary and then taste for seasoning.
- Pour into heated bowls and garnish with basil. Serve at once.

* Serves 4

Spiced Sweet Potato
with Spice Gin

Gingredients

1-2 sweet potatoes, cleaned and cut in whichever style you prefer
Extra-virgin olive oil
15ml *Ginologist* Spice Gin
1 tsp chilli powder
1 tsp cumin
1 tsp garlic powder
1 tsp cinnamon
1 tsp salt

Ginstruction

- Pre-heat oven to 220°C.
- Mix Spice Gin, a tbsp of extra virgin olive oil and all spices together in a small mixing bowl.
- Lay baking/parchment paper down on a baking tray add spread sweet potato fries out evenly.
- Drizzle mixture over the sweet potatoes, coating them to the desired degree.
- Bake for 25 minutes, or until sweet potatoes are nice and crispy!

* Serves 2-4

Potato & Leek Soup
with **Fl**oral Gin

Gingredients

3 tbsp unsalted butter
4 leeks, roughly chopped (white and light green parts only, discard dark green leafy parts)
3 garlic cloves, peeled and roughly chopped
5 potatoes, diced
1750ml chicken (or vegetable) stock
2 bay leaves
1 large bunch fresh thyme
1 tsp salt
½ tsp ground black pepper
250ml *Ginologist* Floral Gin
250ml heavy/double thick cream
Chives, for garnish

Ginstruction

- Melt the butter in a large non-stick soup pot.
- Add leeks and garlic, cook on low heat, stirring regularly until soft and wilted, about 10 minutes.
- Add potatoes, stock, bay leaves, thyme, salt and pepper to the pot and bring to a boil.
- Turn the heat down to low and cover pot with lid.
- Simmer until the potatoes are very soft, about 15 minutes.
- Fish out thyme sprigs and bay leaves.
- You have two options at this point:
  - Leave the soup in the pot and use a hand-held immersion blender to purée the soup until smooth, or
  - Wait for the soup to cool, pour into a standard blender to purée, once puréed, pour the blended soup back into the pot.
- Add gin and bring to a simmer for 5 minutes, before adding cream and salt and pepper to taste.
- Serve immediately and garnish with chives.

* Serves 4

Prawn & Mussel Soup
with **Fl**oral Gin

Gingredients

½ an onion, chopped
1 tsp garlic, minced
1 tbsp olive oil
1 tbsp unsalted butter
1 tsp red pepper flakes
2 410g can peeled
and diced tomatoes
250ml *Ginologist* Floral Gin
1 tbsp sugar
500g prawns,
cleaned and de-shelled, tail on
400g mussels, cleaned
125ml heavy/double thick cream
64g parmesan cheese, grated
64g fresh basil, chopped
Salt and pepper to taste

Ginstruction

- Melt butter and warm oil on medium heat in a medium sized, heavy based pot/pan.
- Gently cook onions on medium heat for about 6 minutes, until soft and fragrant. Then add garlic and chilli and cook 2 minutes further.
- Add tomatoes and sugar and cook for 5 minutes.
- Remove from heat and either use an immersion (hand held) blender, or allow to cool and pour sauce into a standard blender, and blend until sauce is smooth.
- Return to the pot, add gin and bring to a boil for about 30 seconds.
- Close lid and allow to simmer for 15 minutes, stirring regularly.
- During the last 5 minutes of simmering, add the mussels and return lid. Two minutes after that, add the prawns, and return lid.
- Turn off the heat and stir in basil, cream and parmesan cheese.
- Add salt and pepper to taste.
- Discard any mussels that did not open during the cooking process.
- Serve immediately.

* Serves 4

Puff Pastry Straws
with **Ci**trus Gin

Gingredients

75g sundried tomatoes
50g olives
25g olives tapenade
1 tsp dried Italian herbs
15ml *Ginologist* Citrus Gin
Egg wash
Puff pastry (store bought is fine)

Ginstruction

- Chop the sundried tomatoes and olives.
- Add the olive tapenade, gin and herbs and mix.
- Cut the puff pastry into two.
- Spread the tomato and olive mixture onto one half, and place the other half on top.
- Roll out gently to get the pastry to stick.
- Brush with the egg wash.
- Cut into strips.
- Place onto a baking tray prepared with spray and cook.
- Twist the strips and place onto the tray. egg wash again.
- Bake at 200°C for 10-12 minutes until browned and crunchy.

Vegetable Spring Rolls in Rice Paper

with **Fl**oral Gin

Gingredients

1 yellow bell pepper
1 green bell pepper
1 red bell pepper
60g julienne carrots
60g strips of baby corn
60g green beans
2 cloves garlic
Rice paper
50ml olive oil
50ml balsamic vinegar
10ml lime juice
30ml *Ginologist* Floral Gin

Ginstruction

- Cut the bell peppers into strips.
- Place some olive oil and butter in a frying pan.
- Add the chopped garlic and all the vegetables.
- Sauté until the vegetables are soft but have a crunch.
- Take off the heat and add 10ml of the Floral gin and cover the vegetables.
- Take out the rice paper and follow the instructions on the packaging.
- Place the vegetables in the rice paper and fold.

Dressing

- Combine the olive oil, balsamic vinegar, lime juice and Floral gin and pour into a small bowl.

* Serves 4

Salmon Mousse
with Spice Gin

Gingredients

300g smoked salmon strips
500g cream cheese
50ml whipping/heavy/double cream
1 tsp dried dill
20ml *Ginologist* Spice Gin
Salt and pepper to taste

Ginstruction

- Place the smoked salmon and cream cheese in a food processor and blitz until combined.
- Add the cream, dill, gin and salt and pepper and blitz until combined.
- Remove from the food processor and spoon into a glass bowl.
- Cover with cling film/plastic wrap and rest in the fridge until needed.

* Serves 4

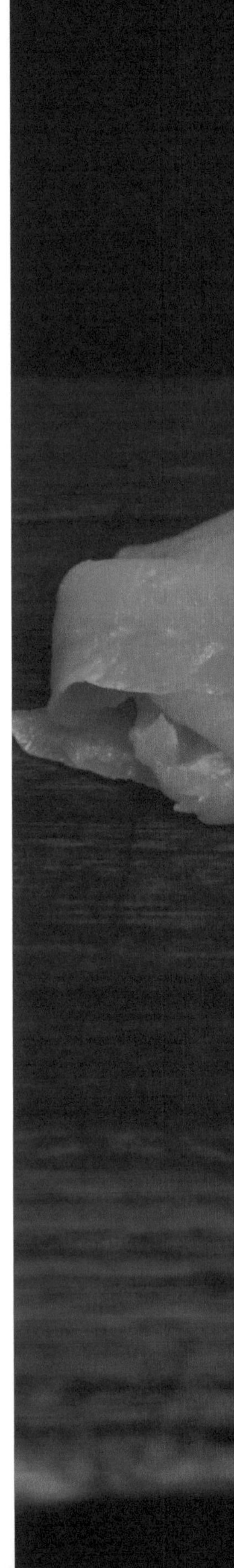

Ginchup
with Spice Gin

Gingredients

2 cans peeled whole tomatoes
200ml tonic water
125ml brown grape vinegar
2 cloves chopped garlic
10ml ground cloves
1 tbsp whole grain mustard
1 tbsp Worcestershire sauce
30ml *Ginologist* Spice Gin
Salt and pepper to taste

Ginstruction

- Add a dash of olive oil to a large stock pot. fry the garlic and add the cans of tomatoes.
- Use some of the tonic water to swirl in the tins and pour into the pot.
- Add the ground cloves, mustard, tonic water, Worcestershire sauce, vinegar, salt and pepper.
- Cook on high until it starts to bubble, take it off the heat and mash the tomatoes.
- Lower the heat and simmer for 45-60 minutes, until it is reduced and thickens.
- Add the gin and mix through. Pour into a blender and blend to desired consistency.

Hint: Serve with Sweet Potato Fries

* Serves 4

Salmon Ceviche
with Citrus Gin

Gingredients

500g fresh sushi grade salmon, diced

1 red bell pepper, diced

1 poblano pepper, minced (remove seeds for less heat)

1 shallot, diced

Juice of 4 limes

Juice of 1 orange

2 tbsp *Ginologist* Citrus Gin

1 small bunch coriander, chopped

Salt and pepper to taste

1 avocado, smashed

Crunchy taco shells to serve ceviche on

Ginstruction

- Combine all ingredients, except for the avocado and tacos, in a bowl and let marinade for 5 minutes if you like your salmon rare, or a few minutes more if you prefer it a little more 'done'.
- Spread a chunk of avocado on each taco, then top with salmon mixture.
- Garnish with remaining coriander.

* Serves 10-12

Boerewors Croquettes
with Spice Gin

Gingredients

75ml *Ginologist* Spice Gin
About **120g** boerewors, finely chopped
100g butter
100g plain flour (plus **40g** plain flour, extra)
375ml full cream milk
2 tbsp chopped fresh parsley
2 eggs, lightly whisked
160g fresh breadcrumbs
Olive oil

Ginstruction

- Grill the boerewors in a non-stick frying pan over high heat until crisp. Set aside.
- Melt the butter in a saucepan over medium heat until fully melted.
- Stir in the flour for 1 minute. Stir in a third of the milk.
- Gradually stir in the rest of the milk until the mixture thickens.
- Stir over high heat until very thick.
- Stir in the boerewors, gin and parsley. Season with black pepper.
- Transfer to a shallow container. Allow to cool for 5 minutes before.
- Roll boerewors mixture into little round croquettes of any size you like.
- Roll in flour, dip in egg and then in breadcrumbs.
- Add oil to a large saucepan to come 5cm up the side of the pan. Cook croquettes, in 3 batches, turning occasionally, until golden and heated through.
- Transfer to a tray lined with paper towel.

* Serving varies depending on size of croquettes

Greek Salad with Soy Dressing
with Citrus Gin

Gingredients

Any salad of your choosing, I used a store bought Greek salad
75ml freshly squeezed lime juice
25ml *Ginologist* Citrus Gin
3 tbsp soy sauce
1 tsp tabasco sauce
1 small brown onion, finely chopped
One 3cm piece fresh ginger, peeled and finely chopped
1 clove garlic, finely chopped or minced
2 tsp honey
¼ tsp freshly ground black pepper
75ml cup extra-virgin olive oil

Ginstruction

- Simply add all ingredients into a large glass bowl, minus the olive oil, and slowly mix in the olive oil until the mixture emulsifies.

Prawn & Mango Salad
with Floral Gin

Gingredients

150g cocktail prawn shelled, deveined and tails removed
(store bought is fine)
150g mango chopped up
300g mixed salad leaves (romaine/cos lettuce, butter lettuce, baby spinach, wild rocket)
100g cocktail tomatoes
50g feta cheese crumbed
50g cucumber slices
100g sliced bell peppers
50g julienned carrots
½ chopped red onion
50ml *Ginologist* Floral Gin
7½ml chopped ginger
30ml olive oil
30ml balsamic vinegar
1 tbsp lime juice

Ginstruction

- Place the prawns in 30ml of the gin. place the salad leaves in a bowl.
- Top with the tomatoes, cucumber slices, bell peppers, carrots and the prawns. top with the crumbled feta chopped mango.
- Add the prawns. Top with the crumbled feta.

Dressing:

- Add the oil, vinegar, lime juice, ginger and remaining gin and mix.
- Pour on top of the salad and serve.

* Serves 4-6

Flame-grilled Spicy Chicken Wing Skewers

with **Fl**oral & **S**pi**c**e Gin

Gingredients

2 brown onions, finely chopped
2 garlic cloves, roughly chopped
2cm piece fresh ginger, peeled, roughly chopped
2 long red chillies, roughly chopped
500g chicken wings
50ml cup soy sauce
Non-stick cooking spray
25ml *Ginologist* Spice Gin
15ml *Ginologist* Floral Gin
250ml can Malaysian satay sauce (see below)
125g cup dry roasted peanuts (unsalted)
250ml water
1 tbsp sweet soy sauce (Kecap Manis)
½ tbsp brown sugar
20g tsp salt
75ml olive oil
1 heaping tbsp tamarind paste

Ginstruction

Satay Sauce

- Mix together peanuts (crushed), water, 1 **tbsp** soy sauce, brown sugar, Floral gin, salt, 75ml olive oil and tamarind paste in a saucepan and stir over medium heat for 5 minutes, or until smooth.

Skewers

- Place brown onions, garlic, ginger and chilli in the bowl of a processor. Pulse until smooth. Toss chicken, onion mixture, Spice gin and soy sauce in a bowl to coat. Cover with cling film/plastic wrap. refrigerate for 30 minutes.
- Thread chicken wings evenly onto skewers.
- Stack a barbecue/braai to your liking and wait until coals/wood has turned grey or use a gas braai and put to medium heat.
- Ensure grill is no more than 15cms higher than coals/wood/gas.
- Place skewers on grill, turning every 2-3 minutes.
- Cook until deep brown and cooked through fire. serve with satay sauce.

* Serves 4-6

Gin & Biltong Salad

with Spice Gin

Gingredients

A mixture of green salad leaves consisting of rocket, lettuce and baby beet greens
15ml *Ginologist* Spice Gin
4 preserved whole green figs, quartered
8 peppadews/piquanté peppers
250g finely sliced beef biltong
100g blue cheese
Balsamic glaze

Ginstruction

- Arrange the salad leaves on a plate, sparing a few.
- Scatter figs over salad leaves.
- Scatter biltong over the salad.
- Crumble blue cheese over the salad.
- Place last of the leaves on top.
- Mix equal parts gin and balsamic in a small saucebowl.
- Drizzle over salad.

* Serves 2-4

Floral Terrine
with **Fl**oral Gin

Gingredients

150ml *Ginologist* Floral Gin
250ml tonic water
50g caster sugar
Two 11g sachets gelatine powder
15ml fresh lime juice
1kg mix of your favourite summer berries (pre-frozen)
Non-stick cooking spray
Two 1L bread pans

Ginstruction

- Allow the berries to defrost, then mix together carefully so as to avoid breaking or bruising them.
- In a saucepan, whisk together half the gin, all the tonic water, all the caster sugar and all the gelatine until fully dissolved, then add lime juice and the remaining gin.
- Once fully mixed and dissolved, remove from heat and allow to cool.
- Place the fruit in a prepared breadpan.
- Pour the liquid over the fruit and mix gently.
- Cover the pan with cling film/plastic wrap and put in fridge.
- Leave in fridge overnight.
- When ready to serve, dip the pan in warm water briefly and remove with a sharp knife.
- Best enjoyed with whipped cream or gelato.

* Serves 4-6

Cool Citrus Tzatziki
with Citrus Gin

Gingredients

20ml *Ginologist* Citrus Gin
2 English cucumbers
500ml plain yoghurt
10ml mint jelly powder
5ml crushed fresh garlic
300ml hot water
Salt to taste
50g rocket
20g beetroot sprouts
Cocktail pita breads
Cherry tomatoes
Cucumber curls and lemon half-slices

Ginstruction

- Grate the unpeeled cucumbers. Transfer into a sieve supported over a bowl, and press firmly to extract all excess moisture
  *Do not throw out the drained liquid.
- Gently combine the yoghurt, drained cucumber, crushed garlic and mint jelly in a mixing bowl.
- Measure the hot water into a measuring jug and stir in the jelly powder until dissolved.

* Serves 4

Pork Belly Loaf
with **Spice** Gin

Gingredients

250g pork belly, finely minced
1 egg
250ml double/heavy cream
150ml *Ginologist* Spice Gin
Twist of lemon
Rocket
2 tsp ground all spice
1 tsp dried oregano
3 garlic cloves
Salt and ground black pepper
Breadpan
Non-stick cooking spray

Ginstruction

- Crush garlic gloves finely and mix together with salt until it forms a paste.
- Mix together all Gingredients [except the cream and egg] and leave in the fridge for a couple of hours.
- Prepare a breadpan, or a loafpan, with non-stick cooking spray.
- Mix the egg and cream together by beating it until smooth.
- Mix them with the Gingredients left in the fridge and pack them into the breadpan.
- Spread butter on top and bake for 1 hour at 200°C.
- Allow to cool.
- Garnish with rocket and a twist of lemon before serving.

* Serves 4-6

Rose Potato Bake
with **Fl**oral Gin

Gingredients

50ml *Ginologist* Floral Gin
60g butter
32g plain flour
200ml milk
128g grated cheddar cheese
128g grated mozzarella cheese
1.2kg potatoes, peeled, thinly sliced

Ginstruction

- Pre-heat oven to 180°C. Use non-stick cooking spray on a large baking dish (25cm or so).
- Melt butter and gin in a saucepan over medium heat. Add flour.
- Cook, stirring constantly until bubbly, remove from heat.
- Slowly add milk, stirring constantly until well combined.
- Return to heat. cook, stirring, until sauce comes to the boil.
- Add 1½ cups of cheese, stir to combine.
- Arrange one-third of potatoes, overlapping slightly, over base of baking dish. Sprinkle with coarse salt. Spoon one-third of the cheese sauce over potatoes. Repeat twice. Sprinkle with remaining cheese.
- Bake for 1 hour, or until potatoes are tender and top is golden. If top begins to brown too much, cover with foil.

* Serves 6-8

Tuna & Spice Dumplings
with Citrus Gin

Gingredients

2 tins of tuna in brine
3cm piece fresh ginger, peeled, finely grated
2 sprigs of chives (10cm each), finely chopped
1 tbsp soy sauce
25ml *Ginologist* Citrus Gin
½ tsp olive oil
30 Asian rice paper wrappers
Baking/parchment paper

Ginstruction

- Strain tins of tuna and add to a bowl.
- Stir in ginger, chives, soy, gin and oil.
- Place 1 wrapper on a flat surface.
- Spoon 2 tsp of tuna mixture into centre of wrapper.
  Brush edges with cold water. Press edges together to seal.
  Place on a baking/parchment paper-lined baking tray.
- Repeat with remaining wrappers and tuna mixture,
  placing dumplings in a single layer on tray lined with baking paper.
- Pre-heat oven to 200°C.
- Arrange the dumplings to that they won't touch each other if they expand.
- Bake for 15-20 minutes until they start to turn golden brown.

* Serves 4

Floral Tomato Soup
with **Fl**oral Gin

Gingredients

30ml *Ginologist* Floral Gin
2 tbsp extra-virgin olive oil
2 small onions, finely chopped
4 cloves garlic, minced
1 can stewed tomatoes
750ml chicken stock
75g tomato paste
½ tsp ground black pepper

Ginstruction

- Heat oil over medium heat in a saucepan.
- Add onions and garlic to saucepan, stirring for 3 minutes.
- Add tomatoes, gin, stock, tomato paste and black pepper.
- Bring to a boil then reduce heat and simmer 15 minutes continuing to stir until slightly thickened.

* Serves 1

Tomato Preserve
with **Fl**oral Gin

Gingredients

1 shallot, minced
1 tbsp olive oil
1 tbsp butter
250g exotic mix tomatoes (or cherry tomatoes)
2 tbsp brown sugar
78ml *Ginologist* Floral Gin
1 tsp salt
½ tsp red chilli flakes
1 tbsp red wine vinegar
1 tsp fresh oregano leaves, roughly chopped

Ginstruction

- Heat oil and melt butter over medium heat.
- Add shallots and cook for about 2 minutes. Then add tomatoes and cook a further 3-5 minutes, until tomatoes begin to soften and break down.
- Add sugar, gin, salt and red chilli flakes and cook for about 10 minutes, stirring often and pushing down on the tomatoes with a wooden spoon to smash. The sauce should begin to thicken.
- Add red wine vinegar and oregano and stir to combine.

Cheesy Bacon Mashed Potatoes
with Floral Gin

Gingredients

350g potatoes
15ml cream
15ml milk
30ml butter
75g grated parmesan
75g mozzarella cheese
150g bacon bits
5ml chopped thyme
Salt and pepper to taste
40ml *Ginologist* Floral Gin

Ginstruction

- Boil the potatoes and when soft remove from heat, drain the water and mash.
- Add the butter, cream, milk, herbs and salt and pepper.
- Fry the bacon bits in some oil and a little bit of water.
- Add the cheese while the potatoes are still hot and mix through.
- Add the bacon and gin and mix through.
- Sprinkle with fresh thyme and serve.

* Serves 4

Summer Prawn Spring Rolls

with Ginologist **Spice** Mayonnaise

Gingredients

4 rice paper sheets
8 small to medium prawns, fully cooked. Deveined and chilled
½ cucumber, de-seeded and julienned
1 carrot finely julienned
½ small paw paw finely julienned or shredded
Small handful fresh mint chopped
Small handful coriander chopped
Small handful basil torn in pieces
50ml chopped unsalted cashew nuts

For the dipping sauce

6 tbsp store bought mayonnaise
Juice of 2 limes
1 tbsp honey
1 tbsp sesame oil
50ml *Ginologist* Spice Gin
10ml fish sauce
10ml rice vinegar
1 clove garlic finely chopped
1 tbsp finely chopped coriander
1 tsp de-seeded chopped red chilli
Add all the ingredients together and set aside

Ginstruction for spring rolls

- Prepare all the vegetables and keep separated aside.
- Soak the rice paper in lukewarm water for 2 minutes until pliable.
- Separate the 4 rice paper sheets separate from each other, divide all the vegetable in 4 and place in the centre of each wrap. Divide the prawns between the wraps. Fold over the sides first and roll from the bottom up, tucking in the sides tightly.
- Place on a platter with the dipping sauce in a small bowl garnish with fresh coriander and enjoy.

* Serves 4

Mains

- Beef Tataki with Coriander Dressing
- The Manly Man
- Cape Dorado
- Chakalaka Salad
- Citrus Peri-Peri Chicken Casserole
- Chicken Satay Skewers
- Citrus Gin Gammon
- Citrus Glazed Salmon
- Classic Sole Meuniere with Capers
- Creamy Chicken & Mushroom Pasta
- Demi-Glace & Beef Fillet with Truffle Butter Sautéed Exotic Mushrooms
- Garlic, Rosemary & Thyme Rubbed Lamb Chops
- Garlic Parm Potatoes
- Juniper Chicken
- Gem Squash Quinoa
- Gin & Tonic Penne
- Hawaiian & Artichoke
- Indian Lamb Curry
- Lentil & Quinoa Salad
- Chicken Floral Delight
- Pickled Fish
- Pumpkin Tart with Cinnamon Sticks
- Savoury Pumpkin Cheesecake
- Seafood Pasta
- Seafood Pizza
- Seared King Scallops & Miso Coconut Cream
- Asian Style Slow Braised Beef Short Ribs
- Teriyaki Salmon
- Tuna Steak
- Thai Spice Chicken Burger
- Peppercorn Sauce
- Mango & Ginologist Citrus Salsa
- Grilled Lamb Cutlets with Fresh Thyme Rub
- Tomato Chutney
- Lemongrass & Ginologist Floral Gin Chicken
- Steamed Salmon with Green Asparagus
- Smoked Fish Cakes with Herby Floral Gin
- Marinated Prawns with Pancetta on Rosemary Skewer
- 18 & over Pizza
- Beef Pie
- Fennel, Orange & Rocket Salad
- Short Ribs
- Beef Fillet Burger
- Slow Roasted Pork Belly
- Duck à La Lychee

Al fresco dining at Hemingways restaurant

Chef **Kundi**

"Spice up your food with Spice Gin, live life on the tasty side!"

Beef Tataki with Coriander Dressing

with **Ci**trus Gin

Gingredients

200g beef rump, grilled to medium rare and thinly sliced
1 small sweet potato
Oil for deep frying

Ginstruction

- Using a mandolin, slice the sweet potato thinly about 2mm thick and deep fry until golden brown and crispy. Set aside for garnish.

Tataki Dressing

Gingredients

60ml *Ginologist* Citrus Gin
2 cloves garlic
60g fresh ginger
1 lemon zest removed and juiced
1 orange zest removed and juiced
2 limes zest removed and juiced
1 small hand full flat leaves parsley
64g coriander leaves
125ml soy sauce
125ml white vinegar
1 small red chilli
2 tbsp dried mixed herbs
2 tbsp balsamic vinegar
4 tbsp extra-virgin olive oil

Ginstruction

- Combine all the Gingredients in a blender and blend until smooth and all the ingredients are combined. Season to taste and set aside.

* Serves 2

The Manly Man
with Spice Gin

Gingredients

30ml *Ginologist* Spice Gin
350g beef sirloin steak
50ml cup soy sauce
2 tbsp worcestershire sauce
3 tbsp minced garlic
1 tsp garlic powder
1 tsp mustard powder
2 tsp onion marmalade
Braai/barbecue wood
Firelighters

Ginstruction

- Mix together all ingredients in a small bowl.
- Marinade steak with the mixture.
- Light the fire and allow wood to burn through nicely until ready.
- Place griddle 15-20 cm above the fire.
- Braai/grill for 2 minutes before turning.
- Repeat until desired doneness is achieved.
- PS - Well done is never a desired doneness.

* Serves 1-2

Cape Dorado

Cape Dorado with White wine Steamed Mussels Topped Gremolata

with Citrus Gin

For the Fish and Mussels

Gingredients

Cape Dorado fillet 200g

1 tbsp sunflower oil

2 knobs butter

4 New Zealand green lipped mussels

½ tbsp Moroccan spice

1 tsp honey

250ml white wine

250ml water

2 cloves garlic

2 sprigs thyme

1 stick lemon grass

Ginstruction

- Firstly spice both sides of the Dorado fillet with. Moroccan spice and drizzle with honey.
- In a heavy saucepan, add wine, water, garlic thyme and lemon grass.
- Bring mixture to the boil and reduce by half.

For the Citrus and Ginologist Citrus Gremolata

Gingredients

2 oranges juiced and zested
1 lime juiced and zested
100ml fresh orange juice
50ml rice wine vinegar
50ml mirin
60ml *Ginologist* Citrus Gin
2 tbsp chopped coriander
2 tbsp chopped flat leave parsley
2 tbsp chopped dill
½ onion finely chopped
2 tomatoes seeded and diced
Salt and pepper to taste

Ginstruction

- Combine all the ingredients, and refrigerate for 1 hour before use.

Assembly

- In a heavy base pan, melt knob of butter with the sunflower oil.
- When hot put the Dorado presentation side down and lightly brown about 45 seconds, turn over and put in a hot oven at 180°C for about 5 minutes.
- While fish is in the oven, warm up the reduced white wine, water, garlic, thyme and lemon grass.
- Drop the mussels in the mixture and poach for 4 minutes until mussels have opened.
- When fish is cooked, top with the cooked mussels and spoon the gremolata over the fish and serve with fresh lemon and dressed wild rocket.

* Serves 2

Chakalaka Salad

A spicy traditional South African salad, with many variations, used as an accompaniment to a barbeque (referred to as 'braai' in South Africa) meal

Gingredients

62,5ml oil
2 onions, chopped
2 green bell peppers, chopped
1 aubergine/eggplant, chopped
1 dried chilli flakes
1 tsp garlic, minced
1 tsp fresh ginger, minced
2 tsp mild curry powder
1 tsp tumeric powder
4 carrots, grated
One 410g tin baked beans in tomato sauce
125ml *Ginologist* Spice Gin
4 heaped tbsp atchar/pickled mango
Salt to taste

Ginstruction

- Heat oil on medium heat then add onions to a large non-stick (important) wok or pan and cook on medium heat for about 5 minutes.
- Add the green peppers and aubergine and cook 5 minutes further.
- Add the garlic, ginger, chilli flakes, curry powder and turmeric powder and cook another two minutes, stirring constantly.
- Add carrots, a little bit at a time, and stir-fry until well incorporated, before adding the baked beans, gin and atchar/pickled mango.
- Stir-fry another 10 minutes.
- Taste and add salt according to taste.
- This salad can be made up to 3 days ahead and served hot or cold.
- Traditionally served with pap/polenta (stiff maize meal porridge) and braai/barbecued meat or at room temperature.

* Serves 6-8

Citrus Peri-Peri Chicken Casserole

with Citrus Gin

Gingredients

10 chicken pieces
2 tbsp flour
1 tsp cayenne pepper
1 tsp paprika
2 tsp chicken spice
1 tsp sugar
2 tbsp olive oil
1 tbsp butter
2 small onions or
1 large onion, chopped

2 oranges (or clementines),
(juiced and rind grated)
One 410g can peeled and
chopped tomatoes
250ml *Ginologist* Citrus Gin
2 cloves garlic, sliced
200ml peri-peri sauce
1 cube/sachet concentrated
chicken stock
4 cloves
Salt and pepper to taste

Ginstruction

- Pre-heat oven to 180°C.
- Mix flour, cayenne pepper, paprika, chicken spice, and heat until golden brown.
- Gently fry the chicken in the oil and butter over medium sugar in a large ziplock bag, add the chicken pieces, and shake to coat.
- Remove chicken and place in a large oven safe casserole dish.
- Gently cook the onions in the remaining fat for about 5-10 minutes.
- Add the orange juice and rind, canned tomato, gin, garlic, peri-peri sauce, chicken stock and cloves and bring to the boil for 30 seconds.
- Taste the sauce and add salt and pepper according to taste.
- Pour the sauce over the chicken pieces in the casserole dish and cover.
- Bake in oven for 1½ hours.
- Remove from the oven and serve piping hot.

* Serves 5-10

Chicken Satay Skewers
with Citrus Gin

Gingredients

2 chicken breasts, thinly sliced
4 tsp crunchy peanut butter
1 tsp chilli powder
2 tbsp soy sauce
60ml *Ginologist* Citrus Gin

For the Chunky Salad
Gingredients

½ onion, peeled and finely sliced
2 small carrots cut into sticks
½ small cabbage, shredded
Grated rind and juice of **1** lime
1 tbsp olive oil
1 tbsp fresh coriander, chopped
Salt and freshly ground black pepper for seasoning

Ginstruction

- Put the peanut butter in a small saucepan with the chilli powder, soy sauce, gin and 200ml hot water.
- Stir over a gentle heat until combined generously with the satay mix.
- Thread the chicken onto 8 small bamboo skewers and brush in a bowl and drizzle over the olive oil, lime rind and juice.
- Cook under a hot grill for 8-10 minutes, turning occasionally.
- Meanwhile, make the salad. Put in the onion, carrots and cabbage.
- Season and mix together well. Place satay skewer on top of salad.

* Serves 4

Citrus Gin Gammon

with **Ci**trus Gin

Gingredients

2kg gammon joint
1 lemon (thinly sliced)
1 lime (thinly sliced)
400ml tonic water (2 cans)
75ml *Ginologist* Citrus Gin
2 tbsp of the cooking liquid
3 tbsp of red onion marmalade
15ml soy sauce
Extra-virgin olive-oil (1 tbsp)

Ginstruction

- Add the gammon, gin, tonic and sliced citrus to a suitably sized pot. Top it off with cold water.
- Bring it to a boil and allow to simmer. Let it simmer for roughly an hour.
- After an hour, place the gammon on a roasting tray with a rack.
- Mix marmalade, cooking liquid and a dash of olive oil together.
- Pre-heat the oven to 190°C. Score the skin into little blocks about 1cm squared each.
- Marinade the gammon with half the glaze and put into the oven for around 15 minutes.
- Marinade again with remainder of marmalade mixture and leave for another 15 minutes until crisp.
- Remove from the oven and leave to breathe for 10-15 minutes before serving.

* Serves 4-6

Citrus Glazed Salmon
with Citrus Gin

For the Salmon

Gingredients

200g Scottish or Norwegian salmon fillet
50ml *Ginologist* Citrus Gin
50ml Yuzu dressing (available at local Chinese market)
Zest and juice of 1 large orange
30ml of soy sauce
½ **clove** of finely chopped garlic
1 thumb sized piece of ginger peeled and grated

Ginstruction

Combine all of the ingredients and leave in the fridge for 3 hours.

For the Salsa

Gingredients

1 whole blood orange segments only
1 whole grapefruit segments only
1 lime segments only
2 tomatoes de-seeded and diced
2 **tbsp** diced cucumber
2 Spring onions thinly sliced (white parts only)
1 **tsp** chopped coriander
1 **tsp** chopped mint
30ml *Ginologist* Citrus Gin
1 **tsp** mirin (available at local Chinese Market)
Salt and pepper to taste
Handful wild rocket

Ginstruction

Combine all the ingredients together.

Cooking Instructions

- In a hot pan melt a knob of butter and a tbsp of sunflower oil. When butter has stopped bubbling put the salmon in the pan skin side down.
- Lightly press down and leave for about 45 seconds until skin is crispy and edges are golden.
- Turn fish over and cook for another 1 minute. Remove from heat and leave to rest.

Assembly

Serve rested salmon fillet on a clean plate and top with salsa, serve with fresh lemon wedges.

* Serves 2

Classic Sole Meuniere with Capers
with Citrus Gin

Gingredients

2 sole fillets, skinned

3 heaped tbsp flour

Salt and pepper, to season the flour

2 tbsp olive oil

1 large block unsalted butter

Juice of **½** a lemon

2 tbsp *Ginologist* Citrus Gin

2 tbsp small/medium capers

Ginstruction

- Season flour well with salt and pepper, then cover fish in flour mixture.
- Heat oil in a large non-stick pan on high heat, dust excess flour off the fish, and fry the fish for about 2 minutes on each side, until golden brown.
- Remove fish from pan and then wipe off excess fat from the pan with a paper towel.
- Reduce the heat, return pan to the stove, add the block of butter and melt. Just as the butter begins to brown, turn off the heat and add the lemon juice, gin, and capers.
- Mix and swirl with the butter to combine and leave on the stove for a minute more.
- Return fish to the pan and coat with sauce and capers.
- Serve immediately.

* Serves 2

Creamy Chicken & Mushroom Pasta

with **Fl**oral Gin

Gingredients

250g chicken breasts
150g mushrooms
1 tbsp pesto
10ml cream
400g pasta of choice
Salt and pepper to taste
10ml chicken spice
5ml mixed herbs
60ml *Ginologist* Floral Gin
Olive oil for frying

Ginstruction

- Cut the chicken into strips and sprinkle with the spice, salt, pepper and herbs.
- Rub 20ml of the gin onto the chicken and place in the fridge for 1 hour.
- Heat the olive oil and fry the chicken until cooked. Remove from the pan.
- Add a little more oil and fry the mushroom.
- Once cooked add the chicken and mix.
- Add the pesto and cream and toss.
- Take off the heat and add the remaining gin.
- Cook the pasta as per the instructions on the packet.
- Place the pasta into a bowl and top with the chicken.

* Serves 4

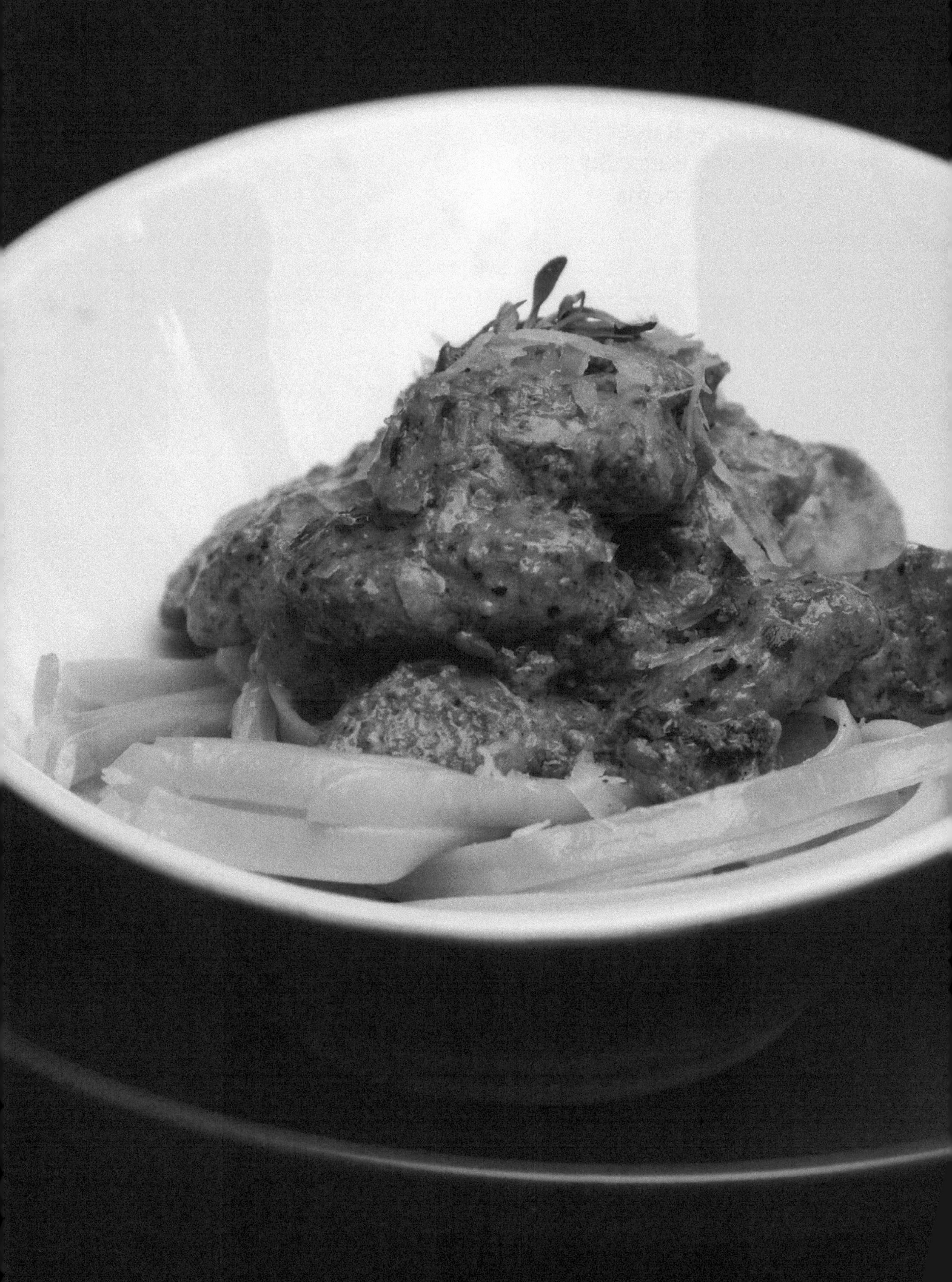

Demi-Glace & Beef Fillet
with Truffle Butter Sautéed
Exotic Mushrooms

Demi-Glace & Beef Fillet with Truffle Butter Sautéed Exotic Mushrooms

with Spice Gin

Gingredients

200g beef fillet seasoned with salt and pepper
150g exotic mushroom
2 knobs salted butter
2 tbsp extra virgin olive oil

Ginstruction

- In a hot griddle pan, melt butter and olive oil.
- Sear the fillet on 1 side for 45 seconds and turn over.
- Cook on a medium heat for 1 minute, remove from the pan and leave to rest this should give you a fillet done perfectly medium rare.
- In the juices of the pan add the mushrooms and cook until softened.

Truffle Butter

Gingredients

150g softened butter
4 tbsp good truffle oil
3 cloves chopped garlic
Zest of 1 lemon
2 tbsp chopped flat leave parsley
2 tbsp picked thyme leaves
1 tsp beef stock powder OR beef stock jelly
60ml *Ginologist* Spice Gin

Ginstruction

Mix all of the ingredients together and roll in a log and cover with film/plastic wrap. Set in the fridge until ready to serve.

For the Demi-Glace

Gingredients

1L beef stock
2 tbsp tomato paste
250ml red wine
250ml *Ginologist* Spice Gin
1 knob butter

Ginstruction

- In a heavy saucepan add the gin and red wine bring to a boil and burn off the alcohol by tilting the pan slightly.
- When the flames have burnt out add the tomato paste and cook for 5 minutes.
- Add the beef stock and reduce the entire mixture by ¾ so it naturally thickens to a coating consistency.
- When ready to serve whisk in the knob of butter for a rich and silky finish.

Assembly

Serve the exotic mushrooms at the bottom, slice the beef fillet and serve on top of the mushrooms, drizzle the demi glace over and enjoy!

* Serves 4

Garlic, Rosemary & Thyme Rubbed Lamb Loin Chops Flambéd

with **Fl**oral Gin

Gingredients

4 lamb loin chops
2 tbsp fresh chopped rosemary
2 tbsp picked thyme leaves
2 cloves of garlic chopped
1 lemon juiced and zest removed
60ml *Ginologist* Floral Gin
Salt and crushed black pepper

Ginstruction

- Combine all the ingredients in a large ziplock bag.
- Massage the meat gently to ensure total coverage of the herb mixture.
- Leave to marinade in the fridge for 3-4 hours.
- On a BBQ make sure the grill is nice and hot, cook the lamb chops to your desired temperature.
- Just before meat is done take 60ml of *Ginologist Floral Gin* and carefully splash the chops, it will catch fire.
- When the flames have stopped, you are ready to season with flaked salt and crushed black pepper, Serve with fresh lemon wedges.

* Serves 4

Garlic Parm Potatoes
with Citrus Gin

Gingredients

1kg small potatoes, quartered
2 tbsp extra-virgin olive oil
15ml *Ginologist* Citrus Gin
5 cloves garlic, crushed
1/3 tsp thyme
1/3 tsp basil
1/3 tsp oregano
64g grated parmesan cheese
Pinch of salt
Pinch of black pepper
2 tbsp butter
2 tbsp chopped fresh parsley
3 sprigs of rosemary

Ginstruction

- Pre-heat oven to 180°C. Lay down baking paper on a large baking tray.
- Mix together olive oil, gin, garlic, all seasoning, cup parmesan cheese, salt, and pepper.
- Place the potatoes on the prepared baking sheet, spreading them out evenly in a single layer.
- Drizzle mixture evenly over the potatoes.
- Break and add rosemary sprigs over potatoes.
- Bake in the oven for 25-30 minutes or until crispy and golden brown. melt butter in a saucepan.
- Garnish with fresh parsley and remaining parmesan cheese.

* Serves 4-6

Juniper Chicken
with Spice Gin

Gingredients

25ml olive oil
4 chicken breasts
1 onion, peeled and diced
1 clove garlic, crushed
15ml parsley
15ml honey
15ml dijon mustard
250ml chicken stock
60ml *Ginologist* Spice Gin
15g juniper berries, crushed

Ginstruction

- Pre-heat over to 190°C.
- Heat oil up in a frying pan.
- When hot, fry chicken quickly until brown.
- Transfer to ovenproof dish.
- Cook for 35 minutes (or until onions soften).
- Blend together all remaining ingredients and pour over chicken.
- Allow to rest for 2-5 minutes before serving.

* Serves 4

Gem Squash Quinoa
With Floral Gin

Gingredients

4 whole gem squash
200g sweet potato
200g pumpkin
300g quinoa
50ml *Ginologist* Floral Gin
50g grated mozzarella

Ginstruction

- Boil the gem squash until soft.
- Chop up the sweet potato and butternut and boil until soft.
- Cook the quinoa as per the instructions on the box.
- Scoop out the flesh from the gem squash.
- Combine and mix the squash, sweet potato and pumpkin, season with salt and pepper.
- Add the quinoa and gin. Scoop into the gem squash shells.
- Sprinkle with the grated mozzarella.
- Place in an oven and grill until the cheese has browned and is melted.

* Serves 4

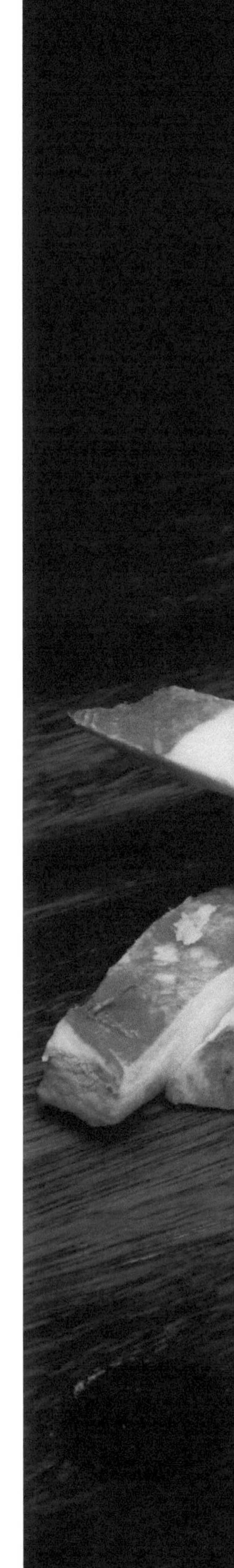

Gin & Tonic Penne

with Spice Gin

Gingredients

1 tbsp olive oil
20ml *Ginologist* Spice Gin
1 red onion, finely chopped
1 can crushed tomatoes
1⁄3 tsp dried oregano
1/3 tsp dried basil
1 tsp salt
½ tsp chilli flakes
50g butter
300g small white mushrooms, thinly sliced
½ tsp ground black pepper
60ml *Ginologist* Spice Gin
1 can (220ml) Indian tonic
750ml double cream
1 tbsp Himalayan salt
250g penne pasta
32g parmesan cheese

Ginstruction

- Heat the oil in a large saucepan. When hot, sauté the onions until golden brown, about 5 minutes.
- Add crushed tomatoes to the saucepan.
- Stir in the oregano, basil, salt and pepper and simmer 1 hour to concentrate flavours.

- While the sauce is cooking, heat 4 tbsp of the butter in a skillet over medium heat.
- Sauté the mushrooms and hot pepper flakes until the mushrooms are golden.
- Carefully add the vodka and simmer for 5 minutes to cook off the alcohol.
- Add the heavy cream and bring to a simmer. pour the cream mixture into the tomato purée. Stir to mix.
- Keep the sauce warm while cooking the pasta.
- Add the Himalayan salt to 6 quarts of water.
- Bring to a rolling/rapid boil.
- Add pasta to boiling water. cook uncovered until pasta is al dente, about 12 minutes. Drain well.
- Melt the remaining 4 tbsp of butter in a large skillet.
- Stir in pasta to glaze, then add Parmesan cheese and mix thoroughly.
- Stir in 1/3 of the sauce and mix with the pasta. Divide among the plates. Top each plate with some additional sauce. Pass remaining sauce and additional cheese at the table.

* Serves 2

Hawaiian &
Artichoke Pizza
with **Fl**oral Gin

Gingredients

1 large store bought pizza base
Grated cheddar and mozzarella cheese,
measured according to preference
128g pineapple, chopped
128g ham, chopped
128g artichokes, roughly chopped
125ml *Ginologist* Floral Gin

Ginstruction

- Mix pineapple, ham, artichokes and gin in a bowl, mix together, and allow to infuse for 30 minutes in the refrigerator.
- Pre-heat oven according to the instructions on the pizza base.
- Layer pizza base with cheese, and then gin infused toppings.
- Bake in the oven for 5-10 minutes, or as per instructions on the pizza base.
- Serve immediately.

* Serves 4

Indian Lamb Curry
with Spice Gin

Gingredients

1kg lamb stew pieces
2 onions, sliced
2 tsp salt
1 tsp pepper
1 tsp garlic, minced
1 tsp ginger, minced
1 tsp tumeric powder
1 small tsp chilli powder for medium heat (or 2 tsp for hot)
1 tsp coriander powder
1 tsp cumin powder
1 tsp whole cumin seeds
2 sticks/quills cinnamon
2 Cloves
2 Cardamoms
4 rainbow peppercorns
One 410g can peeled and chopped tomatoes
1 tsp Tomato Paste
1 cup *Ginologist* Spice Gin
3 cups Hot Water
4 Potatoes, halved or quartered, depending on size
½ cup vegetable oil
2 tbsp Ghee

Ginstruction

- Place oil and ghee into a large non-stick pot on medium heat and warm until ghee is melted.
- Keeping the stove on medium heat, add onions and cook for about 5 minutes.
- Add cinnamon, cloves, cumin seeds, rainbow peppercorns and cardamom, and cook 5 minutes further.
- Add lamb, turmeric, ginger, garlic and salt.
- Cook for about 30 minutes, stirring often.
- Add chilli powder, coriander powder, cumin powder, pepper, tomato paste, canned tomatoes and gin and cook for 10 minutes, stirring often.
- Add water and potatoes and simmer until potatoes are soft and sauce thickened, about 20 minutes.
- Serve with plain Basmati rice.

* Serves 4

Lentil &
Quinoa Salad
with Citrus Gin

Gingredients

200g cous cous
200g quinoa
150g lentils (tinned)
50ml *Ginologist* Citrus Gin
100g feta
100g sundried tomatoes
50g olives

Ginstruction

- Make the cous cous as per the instructions on the box.
- Make the quinoa as per the instructions on the box.
- Mixed the cous cous, quinoa and lentils together.
- Chop up the feta, sundried tomatoes and olives.
- Toss in the *Ginologist* Citrus gin.
- Mix the vegetables (and the gin) with the cous cous and lentils.
- Serve.

* Serves 4

Chicken Floral Delight
with **Fl**oral Gin

Gingredients

4 lean chicken fillets
200g mayonnaise
75ml apple cider vinegar
50ml lemon juice
25ml *Ginologist* Floral Gin
1 tbsp minced garlic
1 tbsp fresh grated horseradish
1 tsp ground black pepper
½ tbsp dijon mustard
1 tsp salt
½ tsp cayenne pepper

Ginstruction

- Mix together the mayonnaise, vinegar, lemon juice, gin, garlic, horseradish, blackpepper, mustard, salt and cayenne pepper thoroughly.
- In a large dish, place chicken fillets and marinade with above mix.
- Allow to stand for 1 hour.
- Whilst marinating, start the fire (either wood or coal) and allow to burn until wood/coal is no longer producing thick smoke and coals have gone grey and are red hot.
- Braai/grill each side for 3-5 minutes before turning over, being careful not to scorch or burn the meat.
- When ready, place chicken on the grill 25-30 above the coals/fire.
- Repeat until chicken is cooked through or to desired doneness.

* Serves 2-4

Pickled Fish
with **Fl**oral Gin

Pickled Fish is a traditional South African Recipe (the exact origins of which remain contentious), where fish is pickled in vinegar and flavoured with curry spices

Gingredients

800g skinless hake or kingklip fillets
1 tbsp oil
250g flour, to coat fish
Salt and pepper, to season flour
6 bay leaves
2 onions, cut into rings
125ml brown spirit vinegar
250ml water
200ml brown sugar
1 tbsp turmeric powder
3 tbsp curry powder
1 tsp salt
10 whole black or mixed peppercorns
1 tsp ground ginger
125ml *Ginologist* Floral Gin
1 heaped tbsp brown onion soup, mixed with a little water to form a smooth paste

Ginstruction

- Season flour well with salt and pepper.
- Dust hake in seasoned flour and fry in hot oil until golden brown and cooked through.
- Remove fish from pan and set aside on roller towel to absorb excess oil.

- In a separate pot, boil vinegar, water, bay leaves, peppercorns, sugar, turmeric, curry powder, ground ginger and salt for about 5 minutes.
- Lower heat, add onions and cook for about 10 minutes further.
- Add gin and brown onion soup paste and cook for a few minutes more, allowing sauce to thicken.
- Add cooked fish and let it simmer in the sauce for 3-5 minutes.
- You may serve immediately or refrigerate for a day or two before serving, to allow the flavours to fully develop.

* Serves 6

Pumpkin Tart with Cinnamon Sticks

with **Fl**oral Gin

Gingredients

1kg chopped pumpkin
250ml water
250ml *Ginologist* Floral Gin
150g soft unsalted butter
3 eggs, at room temperature
125ml heavy/double thick cream
43g sugar
1 tbsp baking powder
100ml flour
1 tsp salt
½ tsp cinnamon powder

Ginstruction

- Cook pumpkin in water and gin mixture, until the liquid has fully reduced, and pumpkin is soft.
- Mash the pumpkin until smooth and free of lumps.
- Decant mashed pumpkin into a measuring jar up to 750ml, and allow to cool.
- Pre-heat oven to 180°C.
- In a large bowl, whisk together sugar, butter, eggs and cream.
- Stir in mashed pumpkin.
- In a separate bowl, mix the remaining dry ingredients then sift into pumpkin mixture until smooth.
- Pour into a 30cm pie dish (for one large tart) or two 24cm pie dishes (for two small tarts) and bake for 35-40 minutes.
- Garnish with two cinnamon quills/sticks.

* Serves 8

Savoury Pumpkin Cheesecake
with Floral Gin

Gingredients

Base

300g plain flour
160g cold butter
1 egg
15ml *Ginologist* Floral Gin

Filling

250g cream cheese
250g mascarpone cheese
200g whipping cream
300g pumpkin
3 eggs
10g dried rosemary
Salt and pepper to taste
35ml *Ginologist Floral Gin*

Ginstruction

- Place the flour and butter in a food processor and pulse until it resembles bread crumbs.
- Place in a mixing bowl and add the *Ginologist* Floral Gin and egg.
- Combine with your hands.
- Roll into a ball and place in film/plastic wrap and rest in the fridge for 20 minutes.
- Boil the pumpkin.
- Once soft, remove from the water and add the rosemary, salt and pepper, and mash.
- Place the mascarpone and cream cheese and mix in a mixing bowl using the paddle attachment, until combined.
- Add the cream and mix until combined.
- Add the mashed pumpkin and mix until combined.
- Add the gin and mix until combined.
- Spray a 24cm spring form tin with spray and cook.
- Roll out the pastry and place at the bottom of the pan.
- Using a fork, prick the pastry. Pour the filling onto the pastry.
- Bake in a water bath at 180°C for 60 minutes or until its golden brown a skewer comes out clean and the filling is still jiggly.
- Leave in the water bath with the door ajar for 90 minutes.
- Then place the cheesecake in the fridge overnight.

* Serves 4-6

Seafood Pasta
with **Fl**oral Gin

Gingredients

350g mixed seafood
6 tomatoes grated
2 tbsp tomato purée
1 sprig fresh thyme
1 sprig fresh rosemary
5 basil leaves chopped
2 onions sliced
4 cloves chopped garlic
Salt and pepper to taste
30ml olive oil
60ml *Ginologist* Floral Gin
500g Pasta of choice

Ginstruction

- Pour the olive oil into a pan with the onions and the garlic and sauté until the onions have softened.
- Add the chopped tomatoes, tomato purée, chopped herbs, salt and pepper.
- Let it simmer on low heat for 45-60 minutes until it is cooked through.
- Pour half the gin over the seafood and place in the fridge for 15 minutes.
- Add the seafood with the gin and cook for an additional 15-20 minutes.
- Take off the heat and add the remaining gin and mix through.
- Cook the pasta according to the instructions on the packet.
- Add the cooked pasta to the pasta sauce and mix using tongs.
- Serve with grated parmesan cheese.

* Serves 4

Seafood Pizza
with Citrus Gin

Gingredients

2 readymade pizza base
200g mixed seafood
100ml tomato paste
2 grated tomatoes
5ml dried Italian herbs
10ml olive oil
1 clove chopped garlic
½ sliced onion
30ml *Ginologist* Citrus Gin
Grated mozzarella
Grated parmesan

Ginstruction

- Pour the olive oil into a pan with the onions and the garlic and sauté until the onions have softened.
- Add the grated tomato and herbs and cook for 15 minutes.
- Pour half the gin over the sea food and let it sit for 30 minutes.
- Add the seafood and cook for additional 12 minutes until the seafood is cooked through.
- Add the remaining gin and mix to combine. Take off the heat.
- Spread the tomato paste onto the pizza based.
- Place the cooked seafood onto the pizza.
- Sprinkle with the grated mozzarella cheese.
- Bake in an oven at 180°C for 12-15 minutes.
- Sprinkle with the grated parmesan.
- Keep the tomato sauce and use as a gravy for other dishes.

* Serves 2-4

Seared King Scallops & Miso Coconut Cream

with Spice Gin

Gingredients

3-5 king scallops (available at any good fishmonger)
1 stick of butter or 50g
1 tin coconut cream
150ml heavy/double cream
1 tsp miso paste (available at local Chinese supermarket)
1 shallot chopped
Zest of 1 lime
50ml *Ginologist* Spice Gin
Beetroot sprouts for garnish

Ginstruction

- In a heavy based saucepan, combine coconut cream, cream, miso paste, chopped shallot, zest, and gin.
- On a low heat slowly bring mixture to a boil and simmer for 5 minutes.
- Strain cream and set aside.
- In a non-stick pan, warm pan and add butter.
- When butter is melted add scallops and leave for 1 minute until golden crust is formed, turn over for another minute and take off the heat immediately.
- In a deep dish bowl of your choice spoon the coconut cream and stack the cooked scallop in the cream.
- Garnish with beetroot sprouts and serve with lemons on the side.

* Serves 1-2

Asian Style Slow Braised Beef Short Ribs

with Spice Gin

Gingredients

2kg beef short ribs, cut into squares
240ml jar hoisin Sauce
250ml water
250ml *Ginologist* Spice Gin
62,5ml Chinese rice wine
2 tbsp Chinese five-spice powder
1 tbsp dried chilli flakes
1 tbsp toasted sesame oil
3 cloves garlic, minced

Ginstruction

- Pre-heat oven to 150°C.
- Season meat with salt and pepper, then sear all sides in a non-stick pan on high heat until well browned.
- Place on paper towel while working on the next step.
- Whisk together all remaining ingredients.
- Place browned meat, together with above mixture, in an oven proof dish which is small enough to allow the liquid to cover the meat.
- Place a sheet of parchment/greaseproof/baking paper directly on top of the mixture and seal off tightly (the sheet should actually touch the food), then cover with lid or foil.
- Place in pre-heated oven and cook for 4 hours.
- Remove from oven, transfer meat to another container and allow to cool to room temperature. Once cooled, you may remove the bones from the meat should you wish to (at this stage they should slide off very easily).
- Once cooled to room temperature, place in the fridge to store for 24 hours (or up to 3 days), allowing the flavours to fully develop.
- Remove from the fridge, remove the hard layer of fat that would have formed right at the top, transfer to an ovenproof dish, and reheat, covered with a lid or foil, for 1 hour in the oven at 150°C.
- To serve, garnish with dried chilli flakes and fresh coriander.

* Serves 8

Teriyaki Salmon

Teriyaki Salmon
with Spice Gin

Gingredients

4 salmon fillets
100ml store bought teriyaki sauce
45ml *Ginologist* Spice Gin
Salt and pepper to taste
10ml fish spice

Ginstruction

- Mix 15ml of the gin with the fish spice to create a rub.
- Rub the salmon down with rub.
- Place in the fridge for 3 hours.
- Pour the teriyaki sauce into a saucepan and thicken for 5 minutes.
- Place the salmon in a frying pan with a little bit of olive oil and fry.
- Add the teriyaki sauce and continue to fry.
- Turn over the salmon and continue to cook.
- Add the remaining gin and stir.
- Cook the salmon medium 6-8 minutes or to your preference.
- Take off the stove and serve.

Hint: Serve with the lentil and quinoa salad.

* Serves 4

Tuna Steak
with Citrus Gin

Gingredients

1 Tuna steak, reasonably thick
1 tbsp fresh lime juice
15ml *Ginologist* Citrus Gin
½ tbsp soy sauce
1 garlic clove, crushed
10g Juniper berries, finely crushed
½ tbsp fresh ginger, minced
2 tsp extra-virgin olive oil
1 tsp pepper flakes
Pinch of sugar, Pinch of salt
Braai/barbecue stand, Firelighters, Braai/barbecue wood, Tongs

Ginstruction

- Add all gingredients to a mixing bowl and mix thoroughly.
- Put tuna in a flat-bottom tray and pour mixture over tuna, marinating both sides.
- Light the fire and allow wood to burn through until red-hot and no longer producing thick smoke (usually until colour of wood turns grey).
- Place grill 15-20cm above coals. grill tuna for 2 minutes before turning over.
- Repeat this until both sides have been grilled for 2 minutes OR until it reaches your desired level of doneness.

* Serves 2

GINOLOGIS
Pieter Carte

Ginologist
Chief Distiller

Pieter Carter

"Come on and get up close and personal with an awesome ***Ginspirational*** *Chicken Burger"*

Thai Spice Chicken Burger
with Spice Gin

For burger patties

Gingredients

500g chicken mince
64g panko breadcrumbs
2 garlic cloves, finely chopped
½ tsp red chilli flakes
40ml *Ginologist* Spice Gin
2 tbsp honey
1 small lime
3 sprigs of lemon thyme, finely chopped
Salt and pepper to taste

Cucumber pickles
2 sesame seed buns
Sweet chilli sauce
Mayonnaise
Equivalent 1 cup lettuce
1 onion, peeled and chopped
50ml rice vinegar
16g sugar
1 tsp salt
3-4 thin slices fresh ginger

Ginstruction

- Place baking/parchment paper on a tray.
- Mix the chicken mince, breadcrumbs, garlic, chilli flakes, gin, honey, lime juice, lemon thyme, salt and pepper together and mix thoroughly.
- Once well mixed, shape into two equally sized patties.
- Heat up a frying pan to medium heat.
- While it is heating up, mix together thinly sliced pickles, finely chopped onion, 1 tsp salt and ginger.
- Pour rice vinegar into the pan.
- Pour in mixture and cook for 7-10 minutes until onions turn golden brown.
- Then add a dash of balsamic vinegar and 2 tbsp brown sugar.

- Cook for a further 5-10 minutes, or until onions caramelize, stirring occasionally.
- Put the cooked mixture to the side in a covered bowl.
- Rinse frying pan.
- Heat up frying again to medium heat.
- Add a dash of extra-virgin olive oil to the pan.
- Place patties in the pan and cook to desired doneness (should take about 10 minutes).
- Slice the buns open horizontally.
- The burger is built in the following order from bottom upwards:
  Sweet chilli sauce, lettuce, patty, mayonnaise, caramelized onion mixture, top bun.

* Serves 2

Peppercorn Sauce

with Spice Gin

Gingredients

2 tbsp butter
1 tbsp oil
1 tsp garlic, minced
2 tbsp black pepper, crushed
1 tbsp flour
1 cup demi-glace (or beef stock)
100ml *Ginologist* Spice Gin
1 bay leaf
2 sprigs fresh thyme
125ml heavy/double thick cream
Squeeze of lemon
Salt and pepper

Ginstruction

- Add oil and butter to a non-stick pan/pot and warm on medium heat.
- Add garlic and crushed pepper and cook for about 2 minutes.
- Add flour and stir quickly, for a minute or so, to create a roux.
- Bit by bit, stirring constantly, slowly add the demi-glace, and then the gin.
  Once fully incorporated, add in the bay leaf and fresh thyme.

Peppercorn Sauce

Mango & Ginologist Citrus Salsa

with Citrus Gin

Gingredients

1 large fresh mango, peeled and cut in to small squares
2 tomatoes de-seeded and diced
1 red onion diced
¼ cucumber de-seeded and diced
10g flat leave parsley finely chopped
30ml *Ginologist* Citrus Gin

Ginstruction

Mix all the ingredients together and refrigerate until ready for use.

Assembly

Spread the cooked rump slices evenly on a plate, spoon the tataki dressing over the rump slices and top with mango salsa, garnish with fresh rocket and sweet potato crisps.

Grilled Lamb Cutlets with Fresh Thyme Rub Tomato & Ginologist Spice Gin Chutney, Parsley & Roasted Garlic Risotto

with **Spice** Gin

Gingredients

Four 100-120g lamb cutlets
2 cloves garlic finely crushed
½ tsp dijon mustard
3 tbsp balsamic vinegar
5 tbsp extra-virgin olive oil.
Hand full fresh thyme
60ml *Ginologist* Spice Gin

Ginstruction

- Combine all of the above and refrigerate for 3 hours or more.
- Heat a non-stick griddle pan until it smokes. Place lamb cutlets in pan for 1½ minutes per side.

* Serves 4

Tomato Chutney
with Spice Gin

Gingredients

250g red onions
500g tomatoes mixed stages of ripeness
1 fresh red chilli
75ml red wine vinegar
140g brown sugar
60ml *Ginologist* Spice Gin

Ginstruction

- Peel and finely slice the onions roughly chop the tomatoes and de-seed and finely slice the chilli.
- Put everything in a pan, season to taste and stir to combine well. Simmer on low heat for 30-40 minutes or until jammy. Stored in an airtight container, will last up to 4 weeks in the fridge.

Lemongrass & Ginologist Floral Gin Chicken

with **Fl**oral Gin

Gingredients

4 free range chicken breasts butter fried
½ thumb size ginger thinly sliced
1 small handful fresh coriander
4 stalks lemongrass, green parts removed
1 **tsp** sesame oil
1 **tin** coconut milk
75ml *Ginologist* Floral Gin
1 **head** broccoli, cut into florets
3 **tbsp** lemon infused avocado oil
Sprigs of fresh coriander to garnish

Ginstruction

- Season the butter fried chicken breasts.
- Place the ginger, coriander and lemongrass in a mortar or food processor and mix thoroughly.
- In a frying pan on medium heat, add the sesame oil with the lemongrass mixture and cook for 2 minutes. Add the chicken and cook for 2 minutes per side, add the gin and light with open flame to cook off the alcohol, add the coconut milk and simmer for 5 minutes. Season to taste.
- Steam the broccoli until tender but green. Drizzle with avocado and lemon oil, garnish with coriander and serve.

* Serves 4

Steamed Salmon with Green Asparagus & a Ginologist Citrus Gin Dressed Salad

Gingredients

Four 150g salmon fillets, deboned
1 glass white wine
½ lemon, sliced
1L water

For the salad

4 oranges
2 spring onions, sliced
150g wild rocket
150g green asparagus cut into 2cm pieces

For the dressing

100ml walnut oil
60ml *Ginologist* Citrus Gin
50ml rice wine vinegar
Juice and zest of 1 orange
Salt and pepper to taste

Ginstruction

- Pre-heat the oven to 250°C.
- Boil the water in a kettle, and then pour into a large roasting pan. Add the white wine and the lemon slices. Place a rack on the bottom of the pan and the fillets on top, and then cover with a tight fitting lid or foil.
- Steam for 15 minutes. While steaming, prepare the salad. Cut the peels off 3 of the oranges, top and bottom first. Then cut off the rest of the peel in strips around each one. Gently remove the orange segments.
- Add the segments in a bowl with the sliced spring onions, rocket, and season with salt and pepper.
- In a small saucepan bring about 300ml of water to a boil with salt. Blanch the asparagus pieces for about 4 minutes or until tender. Remove and put in ice water to avoid over cooking.
- In a small bowl, mix the dressing ingredients together and whisk.
- Mix the asparagus with the salad mixture and pour half the dressing over and toss together.
- Place the salad on the plate and top with steamed salmon.
- Drizzle the balance of the dressing over the fish.

* Serves 4

Smoked Fish Cakes with Herby Ginologist Floral Gin & yoghurt sauce

Gingredients

4 medium potatoes
½ onion, finely chopped
250ml coconut oil
1 clove garlic, crushed
2 tins smoked sardines, drained and bones removed
2 tbsp dill chopped
1 tbsp parsley, chopped
Zest of 1 lemon
Salt and pepper to taste
8 tbsp cornflour
2 large free range eggs beaten
128g desiccated coconut

For the Ginologist Floral Gin & yoghurt sauce

60ml *Ginologist* Floral Gin
250ml Greek yoghurt
1 tbsp lemon juice and the zest
2 tbsp parsley and basil chopped
Salt and pepper to taste

Ginstruction

- Cut the potatoes into small equal cubes and boil in simmering water until tender. Mash while until hot. Season and set aside.
- Sauté the onions in 2 tbsp coconut oil until soft and transparent then add the garlic and cook for another minute.
- Mix the fish and mashed potato, onion and garlic mix, herbs and lemon zest. Adjust seasoning.
- Divide mixture into 12 equal balls and form into equal sized cakes. Leave to rest in the fridge for 30 minutes.
- Grab 3 bowls and place the corn flour, egg, and desiccated coconut separately in each bowl.
- Take the cakes and start rolling first in the cornflour then the egg and then the coconut.
- Heat a heavy based pan with balance of the coconut oil and fry until golden brown and turn over to cook the other side until golden.
- For the dressing add all the ingredients together and blend until incorporated.
- Serve at once.

* Serves 3-4

Marinated Prawns with Pancetta on Rosemary Skewer
with **Cit**rus Gin

Gingredients

4 rosemary branches, long and woody
3 cloves garlic crushed
50ml Italian parsley, chopped
50ml extra-virgin olive oil
50ml *Ginologist* Citrus Gin
50ml balsamic vinegar
16 large prawns, peeled and de veined
100g pancetta or streaky bacon, sliced
½ tsp freshly ground salt and pepper.

Ginstruction

- Fire up the barbecue grill or braai.
- Scrape of 90 percent of the leaves off of the rosemary sprigs and cut the bottom end at an angle to make a sharp edge for skewering. Soak the skewers in cold water for 15 minutes.

For the marinade

- In a mixing bowl, add the garlic, parsley, olive oil, gin, balsamic and the peeled prawns. Toss the prawns in the mixture and set aside at room temperature for 10 minutes. Do not marinade for too long or the vinegar will cook the prawns.

- To assemble for cooking, remove the prawns from the marinade, take the long thin strips of pancetta and wrap around from the base of the tail to the top of the prawn.
- After wrapping each prawn, pierce with the skewer at the tail through the top, to keep it from unravelling place 3-4 prawns on each skewer and grill over low heat and be careful that they don't burn. It will only take about 4-5 minutes per skewer.
- Squeeze with fresh lemon on the grill when done and enjoy.

* Serves 2-4

18 & Over Pizza
with **Fl**oral Gin

Gingredients

Pizza dough
Dough roller
Pizza board
300g calamari rings
200g flour
15g fresh yeast
½ tsp cayenne pepper
Pinch of salt
Pinch of sugar
20ml *Ginologist* Floral Gin
200ml tonic water
250ml pizza base tomato sauce (homemade or store bought is fine)
2 medium sized jalapenos
250g grated mozzarella
128g grated cheddar
1 tsp finely chopped parsley
125ml Greek yoghurt
1 tsp tabasco sauce

Ginstruction

- Bring oil to a boil in a sauté pan.
- Mix together flour, yeast, cayenne pepper, salt, sugar, Floral gin and tonic water.
- Drench calamari rings in this mixture.
- Line a small bowl with paper towels (for the fried calamari rings).
- Fry calamari until golden brown.
- Pre-heat your oven to 200°C.
- Roll dough out flat (no thick base pizzas here!).
- Cut dough to size (30cm in diameter or make it square if you're feeling lazy).
- Using a spoon, cover the cut dough with pizza base sauce.
- Then scatter then sliced jalapenos evenly across.
- Sprinkle the top with cheddar and mozzarella.
- Stick in the oven for 10-15 minutes, or until the dough is nice and crispy.
- While the pizza is baking, mix together the yoghurt and tabasco.
- When ready, remove the pizza from the oven and top with calamari and a sprinkling of parsley.
- Drizzle yoghurt and tabasco sauce over pizza. enjoy!

* Serves 1-2

Beef Pie
with Spice Gin

Gingredients

500g beef
150g chopped sweet potatoes
150g chopped carrots
1 chopped red onion
1 chopped shallot
3 cloves chopped garlic
30ml Worcestershire sauce
1 tin chopped tomato
4 grated tomatoes
75ml *Ginologist* Spice Gin
Puff pastry

Ginstruction

- Heat a heavy based pot with butter and olive oil.
- Add the garlic and chopped onions and sauté until soft.
- Spice the beef with preferred spices.
- Add some water.
- Place the beef in the pot and braise.
- Add the tined and grated tomato.
- Let cook for 30-45 minutes.
- Add the sweet potatoes and carrots.
- Cook until the vegetables are soft.
- Let simmer until the vegetables and beef are soft.
- Add the gin and mix through.
- Place into an ovenproof dish.

- Place the puff pastry on top of the beef.
- Make a cross opening on the pastry.
- Ensure that the pastry has stuck to the sides of the bowl.
- Brush with egg wash.
- Cook for 15 minutes until the pastry is a golden brown.

* Serves 4

Fennel, Orange & Rocket Salad

with Citrus Gin

Gingredients

2 oranges
1 fennel bulb
115g rocket leaves
50g black olives
30g chopped pecan nuts

For the dressing

30ml extra-virgin olive oil
15ml balsamic vinegar
1 small garlic clove crushed
30ml *Ginologist* Citrus Gin
2 tsp honey
½ chilli de-seeded and chopped

Ginstruction

- With a vegetable peeler, cut strips of rind from the oranges, leaving the pith behind and cut into thin julienne strips. Cook the oranges in boiling water for a few minutes. Drain. Peel the oranges, removing all the white pith. Slice them into thin rounds and discard any seeds.
- Cut the fennel bulb in half lengthways and slice across the bulb as thinly as possible, preferably in a food processor fitted with a slicing disc or using a mandolin.
- Combine the oranges and fennel in a serving bowl and toss with the rocket leaves.
- Mix together the oil, vinegar, garlic, gin and seasoning and pour over the salad, toss together well and leave to stand for a few minutes. Sprinkle with the black olives and julienne strips of orange.

* Serves 2

Citrus Braised Short Ribs, with Sesame Dressed Radish Salad
with Citrus Gin

Gingredients

700g un-cooked beef short ribs
1½ L water
3 carrots sliced
1 large onion sliced
3 sticks celery sliced
2 cloves garlic chopped
4 sprigs rosemary
Small handful thyme
2½ glasses red wine
100ml *Ginologist* Citrus Gin
3 tbsp tomato paste
80ml worcesterchire sauce
60ml soy sauce

Ginstruction

- Combine all of the above Gingredients in a pot and bring to a boil, simmer with a closed lid for 4 hours until tender.
- Take 500ml of the cooking liquid and reduce until it coats the back of a spoon.

For the salad

50ml soy sauce
80g Julienne carrots
1 tsp toasted black sesame seeds
2 tsp sesame oil
1 tomato de-seeded and diced
2 tbsp diced cucumber
2 medium sized radishes
2 stems spring onion
white part only sliced
Handful wild rocket
Handful beetroot sprouts
Juice of 1 lime
Salt and pepper to taste

Combine all the Gingredients and chill in the fridge

Serving suggestions

Warm ribs and coat with reduced brazing liquid. Serve salad on the side.

* Serves 2

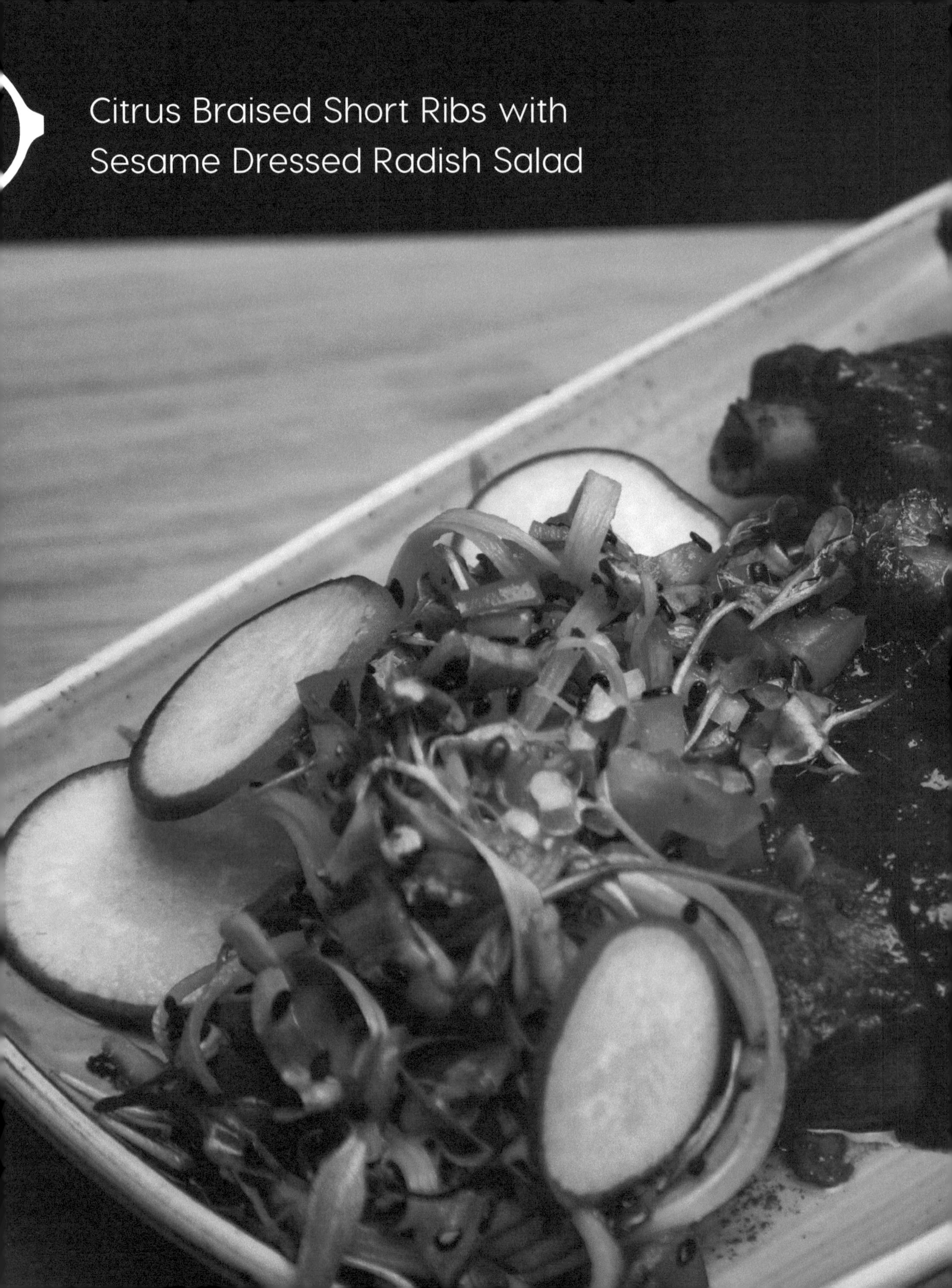
Citrus Braised Short Ribs with
Sesame Dressed Radish Salad

Beef Fillet Burger
with **S**pi**c**e Gin

Gingredients

For fillet

120g beef fillet
Salt and pepper to taste
60ml *Ginologist* Spice Gin

For pesto

128g fresh basil leaves
32g grated parmesan cheese
62,5ml olive oil
32g pine nuts
1 garlic clove, crushed
Salt and pepper to taste

Ginstruction

- Place basil and pine nuts in food processor and pulse several times.
- Add garlic and parmesan and pulse several times.
- While food processor is running, slowly add olive oil, then add salt and pepper.

For sundried tomato

You can buy ready made

Garlic aioli

2 egg yolks
1 bulb garlic (roasted)
1 tsp grian mustard
1 tbsp lemon juice
62,5ml water
125ml sunflower oil
Pinch of cayenne pepper
Salt to taste

Ginstruction

Place eggs, garlic, mustard, lemon juice, water and cayenne pepper in bowl of food processor and blitz, while machine is running add oil at a steady stream until the mixture is emusified.

To assemble

1 burger bun, wild rocket, sundried tomato, aioli, pesto, fillet cooked to your preference, parmesan shaving.

* Serves 1

Slow-Roasted Pork Belly
with Citrus Gin

Gingredients

1kg pork belly
1 tbsp Himalayan salt
8 baby potatoes
1 head of lettuce
1 orange
A pinch of sugar and table salt

The Marinade

60ml *Ginologist* Citrus Gin
80g runny honey
1 tbsp red wine vinegar
60ml plum simple syrup
2 tbsp all spices
200g cherries

Ginstruction

- Mix the marinade. marinade the pork in an oven-safe dish.
- Leave overnight in fridge to marinade. pre-heat the oven to 220°C.
- Rub the pork thoroughly with the Himalayan salt.
- Quarter the baby potatoes and lay them down in the pan neck until the next day.
- Roast for 30 minutes, then turn the heat down to 150°C and roast the pork and baste them along with the pork.
- Turn the heat up for 5-10 minutes to crisp the scored skin for 2½-3 hours.
- Remove the pork and potatoes from the oven.
- Slice the pork into pieces roughly 4mm thick. Prepare plated with chopped lettuce.
- Lay pork on top of the lettuce. zest orange over the plate.
- Add a dash of lemon juice to the pork. Serve with baby potatoes as a side.

* Serves 4-6

Duck à La Lychee
with Citrus Gin

Gingredients

For brine

128g kosher salt
4 bay leaves
1 tbsp dried sage
2 garlic gloves chopped
2L water
64g brown sugar
1 tbsp dried thyme
1 tbsp dried basil
1 tbsp black pepper

Ginstruction

- Boil water and salt, set aside until cold. Add all other ingredients.
- Brine at least 4 duck breast for 12-14 hours. When time is reached, take duck breast out and wash it out with running water, dried with a clean cloth.

Confit Duck Bitterballen

Gingredients

4 legs of duck
2 tbsp salt
3 coffee beans
1 bay leave
2L duck fat

Ginstruction

- In the pot put everything together cook at very low heat until the legs are cooked through.

To make bitterballen

128g mashed potato
Confit duck legs (pulled)
zest of orange
2 roasted garlic gloves
salt to taste
panko crumbs

Ginstruction

- Mix everything to form a binding mixture, roll into ball and crumb them.
- Deep fry on order. You can keep them frozen.

To Assemble Confit baby potatoes

You need 12 potatoes, duck fat (enough to cover the potatoes) and salt. Cook potatoes in fat at a low temperature until soft. Keep for serving.

Duck lychee sauce

Gingredients

62,5ml lychee juice
32g fresh lychee
1L duck stock
25ml Gin

Ginstruction

Put everything together in a saucepan and reduce by , adjust the seasoning.

For bok choy

Blanch bok choy in salted water and transfer into a hot pan, toss with sesame oil.

* Serves 4

VAN LOVEREN
L'AVENIR
L'AVENIR

Desserts

- White Chocolate Cheesecake with Burnt Meringue
- Lime & Ginger Panna Cotta with Strawberry Compote served with Matcha Tuile Biscuit
- Chocolatey Bread & Butter Pudding
- Honey & Chamomile Panna Cotta
- Floral Fudge
- Black Forest Yule Log
- Raspberry & Coconut Ice
- Crème Patisserie Filo Cups
- Floral Ginlato
- G & T (Turkish) Delight
- Date, Pomegranate & Pecan Pie
- Apple Streusel Slice
- Grapefruit Lavender & Rosemary Sorbet
- Citrus Bars
- Crêpes Pêche Suzette
- Coffee Chocolate Mousse
- Spiced Orange Bundt Cake
- Passion Fruit Layer Cake
- Spicy Fruit Cake from Siena
- Nougat
- The Day After Cheat Day Cookies
- Chilli Chocolate Spiced Truffle
- Lime Madeleines
- Floral Crumble Pie
- Eton Mess
- Tiramisu
- Elderflower & Lemon Cupcakes
- Ricotta & Cheesecake
- Citrus Fudge
- Citrus Slush
- Strawberry Spice Turnovers
- Blueberry & Thyme Cheesecake
- Colombian Mousse Meringue
- Gin & Tonic Victoria Sponge
- Rose water Crème Brûlée Flamed
- Moroccan Fruit Salad… Gone Wild!
- Gin Tart
- G & T Sorbet

PASTRIES

"And I will **always** love Gin!"

Chef Charlotte

White chocolate Cheesecake with burnt Italian Meringue & Raspberry Jelly

White Chocolate Cheesecake with burnt Italian Meringue, Ginologist Floral & Raspberry Jelly

with **Fl**oral Gin

Gingredients

For the cheesecake

1½ packets nut crust biscuits finely blended
100g butter melted
500g regular cream cheese softened
64g caster sugar
200g white chocolate buttons melted
2 tsp gelatin dissolved in ¼ cup boiling water
½ cup thickened cream

For the Meringue

4 egg whites
Pinch of salt
60g caster sugar
50g icing sugar
2 tbsp cornflour

Ginstruction

- With an electric mixer, beat egg whites and salt until a soft peak is formed.
- Gradually start adding the sugars and the cornflour.
  Beat until mixture is fluffy and silky.

Gingredients

For the Raspberry Jelly

Two 400g punnets of raspberries
250ml cranberry Juice
60g caster sugar
200ml water
6 leaves gelatin sponged in 100ml water
60ml *Ginoligist* Floral Gin

Ginstruction

- Combine raspberries, cranberry juice, sugar, gin and 200ml water.
- Bring mixture to a boil and cook off the alcohol from the gin.
- Blend until smooth with stick blender and pass through a fine sieve.
- Add the gelatin and cool to room temperature.

Cheesecake assembly

Combine biscuit crumb and melted butter and press into the base of a lightly greased 22cm springform pan and chill. Beat cream cheese and sugar using an electric mixer until smooth, beat in the melted white chocolate and melted gelatin mixture until well combined. Add cream and continue beating until smooth. Pour mixture onto prepared base and refrigerate, pour the cooled raspberry jelly on top of cheesecake and refrigerate for 3 hours or overnight if possible. Once the jelly has set, top with the meringue mixture and torch with a blow torch and serve immediately.

* Serves 4

Lime & Ginger Panna Cotta with Boiled Black Peppers, Strawberry & Ginologist Floral Compote, served with Matcha Tuile Biscuit

with **Fl**oral Gin

Gingredients

For the Panna cotta

400ml double/heavy cream
60ml of grated fresh ginger
Juice of 2 limes
Zest of 3 limes
70ml of caster sugar
4 gelatin leaves
60ml *Ginoligist* Floral Gin

Ginstruction

- In a heavy saucepan on a low temperature, pour cream and add ginger, lime juice, lime zest and caster sugar.
- Bring to a slow boil and simmer for 5 minutes.
- Leave mixture in pan for another 5 minutes and strain.
- Take the 4 leaves of gelatin and soften in 1 cup water.
- Once gelatin is softened, add it to the cream mixture.
- Whisk the mixture for 1 minute and pass through a fine mesh sieve into serving glasses or ramekins.
- Put the ramekins or glasses into the fridge and allow to set for 3 hours.

Gingredients

For the compote

2 tbsp crushed black pepper
100ml water
1 punnet fresh strawberries (200g) cut in halves
30ml crème de cassis (blackcurrant liqueur)

Ginstruction

- Take the pepper and cover with 100ml water bring to a boil the liquid will go brown, once the liquid is brown keep boiling for 5 minutes and strain the liquid.
- Repeat the process 10 times. Reserve the pepper.
- In a separate sauce pot, add the strawberries, crème de cassis, sugar, 100ml water, and the reserved pepper. Bring the mixture to a slow boil and simmer for 10 minutes or until soft.
- If necessary top up with water until strawberries are soft. Set aside to cool.

Gingredients

For the Matcha Tuile Biscuit

3 egg whites
180g caster sugar
90g flour
1 tsp vanilla paste
90g melted butter
½ tsp matcha powder (available in any good grocery store)

Ginstruction

- In a electric mixer whisk up the 3 egg whites to a soft peak on a slow speed.
- Gradually add in the caster sugar until incorporated.
- Add the sifted flour and matcha powder.
- Gently pour in the melted butter and mix until smooth.
- Pre-heat the oven to 180°C.
- Drop ½ tsp of mixture on a silicon mat about 10cm apart.
- Bake in the oven for about 6 minutes or until biscuit is set. Remove from oven, if you would like to shape the tuile this is the right time. Find a suitable bottle and gently shape the tuile around the bottle.

* Serves 2-4

Chocolatey Bread & Butter Pudding

with Spice Gin

Gingredients

250g croissants (store bought is fine)
80g butter
500g milk
250g butter
4 eggs lightly beaten
150g granulated sugar
100g dark chocolate chopped
5g cinnamon
5g clove powder
50ml *Ginoligist* Spice Gin

Ginstruction

- Cut the croissants in half and brush with some of the Spice gin.
- Toast in the oven until golden brown and slightly crunchy.
- Mix the milk, cream and half the sugar in a saucepan and bring to a boil.
- Mix the eggs, remaining sugar, cinnamon and cloves and mix until its nice and thick (a liaison).
- Slowly add the hot milk and cream mixture to the egg liaison and whisk continuously.
- Strain the above custard mixture using a strainer or a sieve into a bowl.
- Add the remaining Spice gin into the custard mixture.
- Add the toasted croissants and the chopped chocolate to the custard mixture.
- Soak in an ice bath for an hour (to allow the croissants to absorb the custard).
- Brush a bowl or individual ramekins with melted butter.
- Using a spoon pour the mixture into a bowl or the ramekins, ¾ full.
- Bake in a water bath at 180°C for 50-60 minutes until golden brown at the top and a skewer comes out clean.

* Serves 4

Honey & Chamomile Panna Cotta

with **Fl**oral Gin

Gingredients

150ml milk
450ml cream
4½ gelatin leaves
100g caster sugar
35ml *Ginoligist* Floral Gin
3 chamomile tea bags
35ml honey

Ginstruction

- Bloom the gelatin leaves on ice cold water.
- Pour the cream and milk into a saucepan, add the sugar, honey and tea bags and bring to a boil.
- Take the saucepan off the heat and add the softened gelatin leaves.
- Whisk until dissolved, pour into a chinois to strain.
- Add the floral gin. Pour into prepared ramekins and place in the fridge to set overnight.

* Serves 4

Floral Fudge
with Floral Gin

Gingredients

397g tin condensed milk
100g icing sugar
75ml *Ginologist* Floral Gin
600g of high quality white chocolate, chopped

Ginstruction

- Line a large baking pan with baking/parchment paper.
- Put the chopped chocolate and condensed milk into a large pan.
- Put pan on low heat and stir often so as to not allow ingredients to burn.
- Once melted, add icing sugar and gin and mix well.
- Pour mixture into baking pan and smooth over.
- Put in fridge and allow to set overnight.
- Check that it has set once removed, if not, back it goes for another couple of hours!

* Serves 8-10

Black Forest Yule Log

Black Forest Yule Log
with Citrus Gin

Gingredients

Sponge

4 eggs separated
120g caster sugar
1 tsp vanilla essence
110g flour
30g cocoa
30g melted butter

Filling

128g cherries
25ml *Ginologist* Citrus Gin
125ml cherry juice
32g sugar
250ml whipping cream
½ tsp orange essence
1 tbsp caster sugar

Buttercream Icing

150g butter
30ml milk
192g icing sugar
10ml *Ginologist* Floral Gin
30ml cocoa

Ginstruction

Filling

- Place the cherries, cherry juice and sugar to a saucepan and place on the stove on low heat.
- Wait for the sugar to boil and a light syrup to form.
- Take off the stove and add the gin, and mix through.

Sponge

- Beat the egg yolks until thick and pale.
- Add the cocoa and ¼ of the sugar and the vanilla extract and continue to beat.
- Whip the egg whites with the remaining sugar until it is fluffy.
- Fold the flour into the egg mixture, Fold in the meringue.
- Fold in the melted butter.
- Spread the batter onto a greased Swiss roll tin and bake at 200°C for 12-15 minutes.
- Turn out onto a damp cloth sprinkled with caster sugar, pull away the greaseproof paper.
- The roll up the sponge lengthwise using the cloth to help.
- Transfer onto a wire rack to cool.
- Whip the cream with the tbsp of caster sugar, until it reaches a soft peak.

To Assemble

Carefully unroll the sponge and using a knife or offset spatula spread the cherry syrup onto the sponge. Spread the whipped cream over and sprinkle the cherries on to the whipped cream. Roll up again without the cloth and place in the fridge for an hour.

Icing

- Cream the butter using a paddle attachment until light and fluffy.
- Add the icing sugar, lemon essence, gin and milk and continue to beat.
- Place into a piping bag with a round nozzle.
- Pipe and decorate to make the cake look like a log.

* Serves 4-6

Raspberry & Rose Coconut Ice

with **Fl**oral Gin

Gingredients

350g Icing sugar
385g condensed milk
300g desiccated coconut
½ tsp cream of tartar
20ml *Ginologist Floral Gin*
5ml raspberry essence
7½ml rose water
2½ml lime juice
Pink food colouring

Ginstruction:

- Grease a square pan with spray and cook and line with baking/parchment paper and grease that.
- Mix the icing sugar and cream of tartar.
- Add the coconut to the condensed milk and mix with the paddle attachment.
- Add the *Ginologist Floral Gin*. Add the icing sugar and cream of tartar.
- Divide in half. Add the raspberry essence and red food colouring to one half.
- Add the rose water and lime juice to the second half and mix until combined.
- Add the white mixture to the pan and press down.
- Spread the pink mixture on top of the white mixture and press down.
- Place in the fridge for 6-8 hours to set.
- Once set remove from the pan and cut into squares.

* Serves 4

Crème Patisserie Filo Cups

with Spice Gin

Gingredients

Filo Pastry
300g milk
110g granulated sugar
3 egg yolks
40g cornflour
1 vanilla pod
2 star anise
5 cardamom pods cracked open
35ml *Ginologist* Spice Gin
1 tsp orange essence
15g butter
Chopped up fruit of choice for the topping

Ginstruction

- Make a paste with 80g of the milk, sugar, egg yolks, and cornflour, set aside.
- Boil the remaining milk with all the spices, remove from the heat.
- Slowly stream the boiled milk into the egg mixture and continue to whisk.
- Then pour back into the saucepan and continue whisking on low heat, until it thickens.
- Pour through a chinois.
- Take off the heat, stir in the gin and the butter.
- Spray the muffin pan with spray and cook.
- Cut the filo pastry into squares.
- Place the filo into the muffin cups.

* Serves 4

Floral Ginlato
with Floral Gin

Gingredients

100ml *Ginologist* Floral Gin
125g caster sugar
250ml full-fat milk
250g assortment of summer berries (good quality)
2 eggs (I used extra large)
400g clotted cream

Ginstruction

- Whisk the eggs in a large bowl until frothy.
- Add the sugar gradually and whisk until you're good and tired, but more importantly until it all seems smooth and mixed in well.
- Add the clotted cream and milk to the egg mixture and whisk thoroughly. I found that adding this gradually helped.
- Spoon the mixture into a very large container (2 litres should do) and freeze for 3 hours (an ice cream maker would make life easier).
- Remove and whisk until smooth (resist the temptation to taste… you won't stop).
- Return to the freezer for another 3 hours.
- Repeat this process 3 times (or more if not smooth enough yet).
- Once smooth enough, mix summer berries into the ice cream (I put them through a *Nutribullet*, but you can go halved or even processed to make it smoother, really up to the person making it, though I think smoother would be better here).
- Once mixed in thoroughly, return to freezer until frozen (Same consistency as ice cream, not frozen solid of course).

* Serves 8-10

G & T (Turkish) Delight
with **Fl**oral Gin

Gingredients

8 gelatine leaves
2 level tbsp icing sugar
15ml *Ginologist* Floral Gin
Few drops of pink liquid food colouring
18cm square baking pan
500g granulated sugar
1 level tbsp cornflour

Ginstruction:

- Pour 300ml tonic water into a pan.
- Break gelatine leaves up a bit to make them easier to handle and add them to the water.
- Let gelatine rest in water for a couple of minutes.
- Place pan on low heat and stir gently as gelatine melts.
- Add sugar and stir until it dissolves.
- Bring the mixture to a boil and immediately reduce heat to allow mixture to simmer for 20 minutes.
- Remember to stir occasionally.
- Remove the pan from the heat and stir in the gin and food colouring.
- Prepare the baking pan with non-stick spray and pour in mixture.
- Allow to set overnight. Remove carefully using a sharp knife.
- Dust the top with icing sugar.

* Serves 4-6

Date, Pomegranate & Pecan Pie

with Spice Gin

Gingredients:

Pie Crust

250g flour
160g cold butter cubed
Pinch of salt
15ml water or Gin

Filling

200g sugar
200g butter
2 eggs
100g ground pecans
50g cake flour
75g chopped dates
45ml *Ginologist* Spice Gin
50ml pomegranate juice

Ginstruction

Pie Crust

- Add the flour, salt and butter in a food processor and pulse until it resembles bread crumbs.
- Add the gin/water and mix by hand to form a dough.
- Wrap in film/plastic wrap and place in the fridge to rest until needed.

Filling

- Cream the butter until light and fluffy.
- Add the sugar and continue to cream.
- Add the eggs one at a time, until combined.
- Soak the dates in the gin and pomegranate juice for 1 hour.
- Mix the ground pecans and cake flour.
- Fold into the butter mixture until just combined.
- Prepare a pie pan with spray and cook.
- Roll out the dough to about 4mm thick and line a pie pan with it.
- Pour in the filling.
- Place remaining pecan and pomegranate rubies.
- Bake at 180°C until golden brown and glaze.

* Serves 6

Apple Streusel Slice

with Spice Gin

Gingredients

Base

250g cake flour
50g caster sugar
130g butter
1 egg
1 egg yolk
15ml *Ginologist Spice* Gin/milk

Apple Filling

200g tinned apples
30g butter
10ml cinnamon
10ml ginger
5ml cloves
50g muscovado sugar
150g cream
50g milk
1 egg yolk
25ml *Ginologist* Floral Gin

Streusel Topping

150g flour
70g brown sugar
100g oats
50g butter
7½ml mixed spices
30g chopped pecan nut (optional)

Ginstruction

Base

- Combine the flour sugar and butter in a food processor until it forms bread crumbs. Add the milk, egg and egg yolks and mix to combine with your hands until it forms a dough, be careful not to over mix.
- Roll in film/plastic wrap and place in the fridge to rest for 20 minutes. Roll the pastry out to about 3mm thick. Line a rectangular baking tin with the baking/parchment paper and blind bake at 180°C for 12 minutes.
- Take out the baking beads and bake for an additional 5 minutes.

Filling

- Melt the butter in a pan and add the apples. Add the spices and sugar and cook until a syrup forms and coats the apples.
- Take off the heat and add the gin in a separate bowl. Whisk the cream, milk and egg yolk and place in the stove and whisk for 5 minutes.

Streusel Topping

- Add the all the ingredients into a bowl and mix with your fingers until it forms bread crumbs.
- Place the apples on the base and then pour the vanilla sauce over the apples.
- Bake for 20 minutes at 180°C until the apple custard is wobbly but not set. Take out and sprinkle the Streusel topping on top of the apple custard mixture. Place back into the oven and bake for 12 minutes.
- Take out and cool completely before slicing.

* Serves 6-8

Grapefruit Lavender & Rosemary Sorbet

with **Fl**oral Gin

Gingredients

150g caster sugar
50g glucose
100g water
500g grapefruit purée
2 gelatin leaves
100ml milk
5ml lemon juice
5ml lavender essence
10g chopped rosemary
25ml *Ginologist* Floral Gin

Ginstruction

- Add the water and sugar into a saucepan and sand with your hands.
- Add the glucose, milk, and bring to a boil.
- Take off the stove. Add half the purée and stir until combined. Add the remaining half, milk lavender essence.
- Once combined whisk in the gelatin leave.
- Put into an ice cream maker and follow the instructions.
- Pour into a shallow metal tray, cover and freeze.
- Take out and mix thoroughly every hour and place back in the freezer.

* Serves 4-6

Citrus Bars
with Citrus Gin

Gingredients

For the crust:

12 tbsp butter, cut in small pieces
6 tbsp sugar
192g flour

For the filling:

192g sugar
32g flour
20ml *Ginologist* Citrus Gin
4 eggs
125ml of lemon juice
62ml of lime juice
1 tbsp lemon zest

Ginstruction

- Pre-heat oven to 180°C.
- Blend crust ingredients together thoroughly.
- Line an oven friendly baking pan (medium, 20cm) with baking/parchment paper.
- Flatten crust mixture in the baking pan. Bake the crust for 22-25 minutes.
- Combine the 1½ cups sugar, ¼ cup flour, 4 eggs, lemon juice, lime juice, gin and zest in a large bowl and whisk well.
- Allow mixture to settle while crust bakes.
- Remove crust from oven. Whisk again as you pour mixture over crust.
- Put the pan back in the oven for 20-22 minutes.
- Remove once top has set.

* Serves 4-6 depending on block sizes

Crêpes Pêche Suzette
with Spice Gin

Gingredients

Crêpes

240g milk
120g cream
3 eggs
15g butter melted
20g caster sugar
180g plain flour
Oil for frying

Pêche Suzette

120g butter
45g brown sugar
5ml nutmeg
2 whole star anise
25ml *Ginologist* Spice Gin
50ml peach juice
100ml tonic water
1 peach, sliced
1 nectarine
Sliced grated whole nutmeg for garnishing

Ginstruction

Crêpe

- Pour the milk, cream, eggs, melted butter in a bowl and whisk.
- Sieve the flour and caster sugar and add to whisk into above mixture.

- Strain the batter through a sieve, into a bowl, cover with cling film/plastic wrap and let rest in the fridge for 30-60 minutes, but not more than 8 hours.
- Melt a small amount of butter in a pan.
- Ladle the batter into the pan and cover the surface.
- Cook for about 2 minutes on each side or until bubbles start to form, and it becomes gold brown on the underside.
- Place on a plate and repeat.

Pêche Suzette

- Heat a crêpe pan (preferably) on medium to low heat and sprinkle the sugar, add a little water and caramelize the sugar.
- As it starts to boil slowly add the butter on the outside and move the pan to combine the butter and the sugar.
- Add the star anise and ground nutmeg, shake the pan to combine the ingredients.
- Add the peach Juice and tonic water, and continue to boil and stir until a syrup forms.
- Add the sliced peaches and nectarines and coat through.
- Take off the heat and add the gin, and mix through.
- Add the crêpes to the pan, cover with the syrup and warm on the stove.
- Remove the crêpes and plate 3 at a time.
- Pour the remaining syrup with the peaches onto the plated crêpes.
- Serve.

* Serves 2-4

Crêpe Pêche Suzette

Coffee Chocolate Mousse

with Spice Gin

Gingredients

230g dark chocolate
100g caster sugar
4 egg yolks
500g whipping cream
30ml *Ginologist* Spice Gin
1 tbsp ground coffee

Ginstruction

- Heat 125g of the cream with the ground coffee.
- Pass through a chinoise.
- Whisk the egg yolks until they are pale in colour.
- Add half the sugar and carry on whisking.
- Slowly stream the hot cream into the egg yolk mixture.
- Add the gin and continue to whisk.
- Place on low heat and whisk until it thickens (coats the back of a metal spoon).
- Melt the chocolate.
- Slowly fold the melted chocolate into the custard mixture, and cool.
- Whip the remaining cream with the sugar until it forms stiff peaks.
- Gently fold in of the whipped cream mixture into the cooled chocolate custard mixture.
- Add in the remaining and fold until combined.
- Spoon into glass bowls and chill in the fridge overnight.
- Serve at room temperature.

* Serves 2-4

Spiced Orange Bundt Cake
with **S**pi**c**e Gin

Gingredients

Sponge

220g butter
1¼ cup sugar
3 large eggs
250g flour
1 tsp nutmeg
1 tsp cloves
1 tsp baking powder
1 tbsp candied citrus peel
1 tbsp *Ginologist* Spice Gin
1 tsp orange essence

Orange Syrup

125ml water
128g sugar
125ml fresh orange juice
25ml *Ginologist* Spice Gin

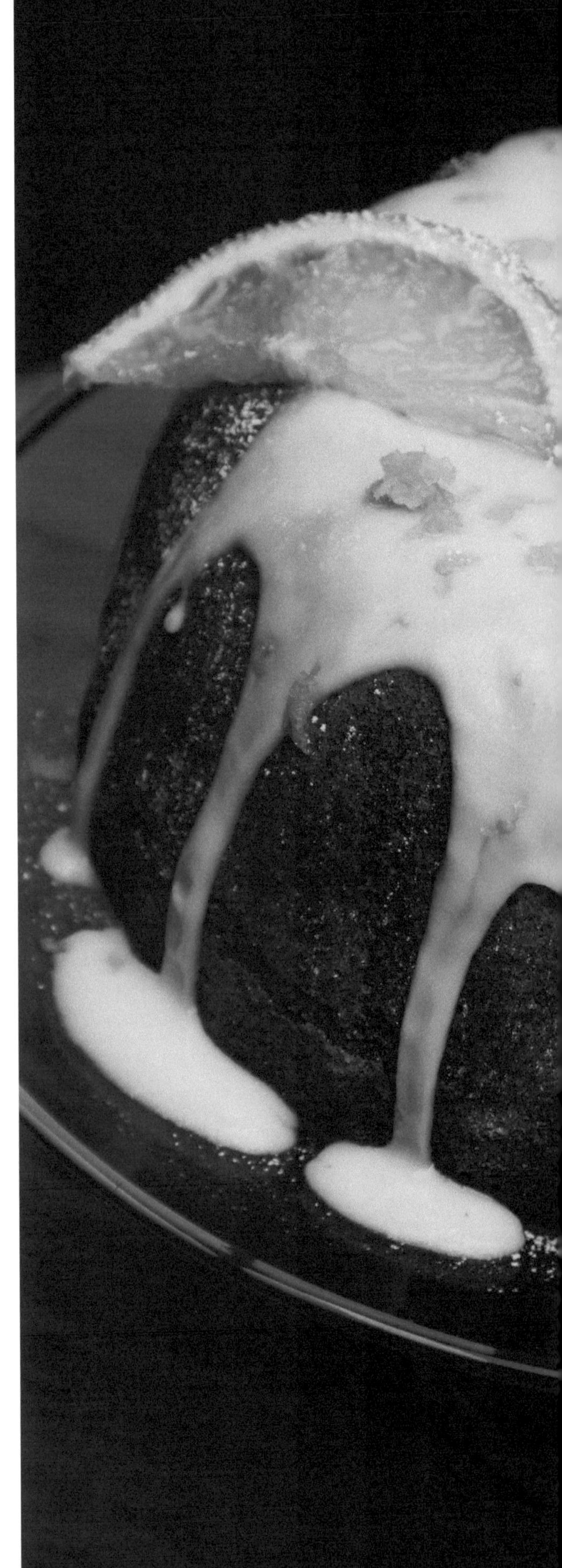

Orange Glaze

192g icing sugar
62ml orange juice
5ml *Ginologist* Spice Gin

Ginstruction

- Heat the oven to 180°C and spray and flour a bundt pan.
- Cream butter with a beater. Add the caster sugar and orange essence.
- Add the eggs one at a time and mix until combined. Soak the candied orange peel in *Ginologist* Spice Gin and mix until combined.
- Mix the flour with the baking powder and spices.
- Add the flour mixture, and mix to just combined (be careful not to overmix).
- Pour the mixture into the prepared bundt pan. Bake for 50-55 minutes, until golden brown and a skewer comes out clean. Let cool in a pan, and then turn out to continue to cool on a cooling rack.
- Add the sugar to a pan, add the juice and water around and sand with your fingers.
- Place on the stove and boil until the sugar has dissolved and simple sugar syrup is formed. Take off the heat and stir in the gin.

Mix the icing sugar with the orange juice and gin

* Serves 4-6

Passion Fruit Layer Cake
with Floral Gin

Gingredients

Sponge

225g baking margarine/butter
250g caster sugar
4 eggs
125ml sour cream
125ml coconut cream
125ml oil
314g flour
1 tsp baking powder
1 tsp bicarbonate of soda
1 tsp salt
1 tsp passion fruit essence
Pulp of 2 passion fruits
20ml *Ginologist* Floral Gin

Passion Fruit Curd

4 egg yolks
80g sugar
cup passion fruit pulp
62,5ml passion fruit juice
125g butter
25ml *Ginologist* Floral Gin

Passion Fruit Coulis

3 passion fruits
64g caster sugar
10ml *Ginologist* Floral Gin
80ml water

Buttercream Icing

150g butter
192g icing sugar
40ml milk
5ml passion fruit essence

Ginstruction

- Cream the butter until light and fluffy. Add the sugar and passion fruit essence and continue to cream. Add the eggs one by one and mix until combined.
- Add the passion fruit pulp. Sift the flour, baking powder and bicarbonate of soda together. Mix the gin, sour cream and oil together.
- Alternatively add the dry and wet mixture into the butter mixture starting and finishing with the dry mixture Pour into 3 sprayed pans.
- Bake at 180°C for 25-30 minutes until golden brown and the skewer comes out clean.

Curd

- In a saucepan add the butter, sugar, juice and pulp (the sugar must melt before it boils)
- Add the yolks into a bowl and whisk until pale white.
- Add the hot mixture into the cold yolks slowly and continue mixing. Put back onto the stove while whisking continuously.
- Cool in the fridge.

Buttercream

- Cream the butter using a paddle attachment until light and fluffy.
- Add the icing sugar, passion fruit essence, gin and milk and continue to beat.

* Serves 6-8

Passion Fruit Layer Cake

Spicy Fruit Cake from Siena

with Spice Gin

Gingredients

225g mixed candied fruits diced.
¼ tsp ground coriander
¾ tsp ground cinnamon
¼ tsp ground cloves
¼ tsp grated nutmeg
50g plain flour
115g honey
70ml *Ginologist* Spice Gin
115g granulated white sugar
Icing sugar for dusting
Butter for greasing a 20cm round cake tin
175g hazelnuts roughly chopped
75g whole almonds roughly chopped

Ginstruction

- Pre-heat the oven to 180°C.
- Grease the 20cm round cake tin with butter.
  Line the base of the tin with non-stick greaseproof paper.
- Spread the nuts on a baking tray and place in the oven for about 10 minutes until lightly toasted. Remove and set aside. Lower the oven temperature to 150°C.
- In a large mixing bowl combine the candied fruits, all the spices and the gin with the flour and stir together with a wooden spoon.
  Add the nuts and stir in thoroughly.
- In a small heavy saucepan, stir together the honey and sugar and bring to a boil. Cook the mixture until it reaches 140°C on a sugar thermometer or when a small bit forms a hard ball when pressed between fingertips in iced water. Take care when doing this and use a tsp to remove a little mixture out of the pan for testing.
- At this stage immediately pour the sugar syrup into the dry Gingredients and stir in well until evenly coated. Pour into a prepared tin. Dip a spoon into water and use the back of the spoon to press the mixture into the tin.
  Bake in the pre-heated oven for 1 hour.
- When ready, it will suntil feel quite soft but will harden as it cools.
  Cool completely in the tin and then turn out on to a serving plate.
  Dust with icing sugar before serving.

* Serves 4-6

Nougat
with **Fl**oral Gin

Gingredients

2 pieces of rice paper
440g caster sugar
200ml glucose
90g honey
90g maple syrup
65ml water
30ml *Ginologist* Floral Gin
2 egg whites
100g butter
100g choice of nuts roasted
60g cherries
60g cranberries

Ginstruction

- In a saucepan add the sugar and water and sand using your fingers.
- Add the glucose, honey and syrup to the water and sugar mixture and bring to a boil until the mixture reaches 130°C.
- In the meantime, whip the egg whites until shiny and glossy and stiff peaks form. Slowly add the sugar syrup the egg white mixture and continue to beat until it thickens. Add in the butter and the gin and continue to whip.
- Stir in the nuts, cranberries and cherries.
- Pour into a cold tray lined with rice paper.
- Smooth over and place the second piece of rice paper on to.
- Put in fridge until set then remove and shape into desired clouds or pieces whichever you prefer, dust with icing sugar and serve with coffee after dinner!

The Day After Cheat Day Cookies
with **Spice** Gin

Gingredients

15ml *Ginologist* Spice Gin
128g salted butter
128g sugar
64g brown sugar
2 large eggs
1 dash vanilla essence
384g pastry flour
2¼ tsp cinnamon
1 tsp baking powder
1 tsp baking soda
½ tsp salt
250g grated raw carrots
Cream cheese frosting
128g chopped raw almonds

Ginstruction

- Pre-heat oven to 180°C.
- In a large bowl, mix butter and sugar (granulated and brown) with a mixer until smooth.
- Beat in eggs and vanilla.
- Mix in cinnamon, baking powder, baking soda and salt and mix thoroughly.
- Add flour and mix until combined. Add in 2 cups of carrots.
- Lay mixture down on a baking tray lined with baking paper.
- Cut cookies to shape using a cookie cutter of choice.
- Bake the cookies for 13-15 minutes or until golden brown around the edges.
- Allow cookies to cool. Frost with the best cream cheese frosting.
- Add chopped almonds to top.

* Serves 4-8

Chilli Chocolate Spiced Truffle
with Spice Gin

Gingredients

200g heavy/whipping cream
1 tsp chilli flakes
400g good quality dark chocolate
15g butter
30ml *Ginologist* Spice Gin

Ginstruction

- Boil the cream with the chilli flakes. Remove the pod and strain the the cream (optional). Mix the gin into the cream and pour over the broken chocolate pieces.
- Let stand for 5 minutes. Mix until it forms a smooth paste.
- Temper the butter into the mixture.
- Place in the fridge for 12-18 hours. Using a melon baller, scoop balls and shape them into your palms.
- Dip in melted chocolate and let stand then serve.

* Serves 6-8

Lime Madeleines
with Citrus Gin

Gingredients

100g of sugar
3 eggs
128g flour
½ tsp baking powder
½ tsp vanilla essence
1 tsp lime zest
10ml *Ginologist* Citrus Gin
cup butter

Ginstruction

- Melt the butter and let cool. Beat the eggs vanilla essence and lime zest until pale yellow.
- Slowly add the sugar while beating and keep beating until the egg mixture is thick and forms ribbons when you lift the whisk/beaters.
- Mix the gin into the cooled butter. Sift the flour and baking powder and gently fold the flour and cooled butter alternatively into the batter.
- Grease the madeleines pan and lightly flour, shake off any extra flour.
- Using a tbsp, scoop and pour into the moulds.
  Bake for 12-15min at 180°C until golden brown around the edges.

* Serves 6

Floral Crumble Pie
with **Fl**oral Gin

Gingredients

60ml *Ginoligist* Floral Gin
135g plain flour
50g crushed raw almonds
150g butter, cubed
135g of sugar (for top)
500g pitted tart red cherries
32g cornflour
128g white sugar (for filling)
1 packet tennis biscuits
250g margarine

Ginstruction

- Pre-heat oven to 180°C.
- Melt margarine in microwave. Crush The Day After Cheat Day Cookies and mix with margarine. Press into a round pie dish.
- Place cherries into a saucepan over medium heat and cook until the juice comes to a simmer, stirring often to avoid burning, for 10-15 minutes. In a bowl, whisk the sugar with cornflour thoroughly.
- Pour the mixture into the hot cherries and juice, and mix thoroughly.
- Add gin and mix thoroughly once more.
- Return to low heat, bring to a simmer (for about 2 minutes), and cook until the filling has thickened.
- Remove from heat and allow to cool down. Pour the filling into the pie crust.
- Put plain flour, butter, almonds and sugar in a bowl and mix well (until crumbly).
- Sprinkle topping so as to cover the filling entirely.
- Bake for 35-40 minutes or until golden brown.
- Allow to cool for 30 minutes before serving

* Serves 4-6.

Eton Mess
with Citrus Gin

Gingredients

Meringue

200g egg whites
150g caster sugar
50g icing sugar
15g cornflour
20ml vinegar
20ml *Ginologist* Citrus Gin

Filling

250g strawberries hulled
30ml *Ginologist* Citrus Gin
15ml caster sugar
250g whipping cream

Ginstruction

- Add the eggs whites, icing sugar, caster sugar, vinegar and gin into a mixing bowl and whip until the meringue is glossy and shining and is in hard peak form.
- Place into a piping bag and pipe individual meringue kisses or one large meringue. Bake at 110°C until dry.
- Switch off the oven and leave the door ajar let the meringues sit overnight.
- Chop up the strawberries and pour the gin over them, let them sit overnight.

* Serves 4

Tiramisu
with Floral Gin

Gingredients

3 eggs separated
100g caster sugar
60ml *Ginologist* Floral Gin
120ml Kahlua coffee liqueur
18 boudoir/sponge finger biscuits
1 tsp vanilla paste
175ml cup cold strong black coffee
150g mascarpone cheese
(at room temperature)
Sifted cocoa powder and grated
bittersweet chocolate to finish

Ginstruction

- Put the egg whites in a grease free bowl and whisk with an electric mixer until stiff and in peaks.
- Mix the mascarpone, vanilla paste and caster sugar and egg yolks in a separate large bowl and whisk with the electric mixer until evenly combined. Fold in the egg whites, then put a few spoonfuls of the mixture in the bottom of a large serving bowl and spread it out evenly.
- Mix the coffee, liqueur, and gin together in a shallow dish. Dip a boudoir/sponge finger in the mixture, turn it quickly so that it becomes saturated but does not disintegrate, and place it on top of the mascarpone in the bowl. Add five more dipped boudoir/sponge fingers, placing them side-by-side.
- Spoon in about one-third of the remaining mixture and spread it out. Make more layers in the same way, ending with mascarpone. Level the surface, and then sift cocoa powder all over. Cover and chill overnight. Before serving, sprinkle with cocoa and grated chocolate.

* Serves 4-6

Elderflower & Lemon Cupcakes
with Citrus Gin

Gingredients

Sponge

225g butter/baking margarine
5ml vanilla essence
192g sugar
3 eggs
750g flour
1 tsp baking powder
1 tsp elderflower cordial
15ml milk
15ml *Ginologist* Citrus Gin

Buttercream Icing

250g butter
750g icing sugar
40ml milk
5ml Lemon essence
5ml Gin

Ginstruction

- Cream the butter and vanilla essence in a mixing bowl until light and fluffy. Add the sugar and continue to cream.
- Add the eggs one at a time. Sift the flour and baking powder.
- Add the flour, milk and gin and mix until just combined. Line a cupcake pan with cupcake holder. Fill to ¾ (approximately 60g). Bake at 180°C for 12-15 minutes until golden brown at the top. Take out and cool on a cooling rack.

Icing

- Cream the butter using a paddle attachment until light and fluffy.
- Add the icing sugar, lemon essence, gin and milk and continue to beat.
- Place into a piping bag with a desired nozzle. Once the cupcakes are cooled, pipe and serve.

* Serves 12

Ricotta & Cheesecake
with Citrus Gin

Gingredients

450g low fat ricotta cheese
1 egg yolk
120ml double/heavy cream
2 eggs
80ml *Ginologist* Citrus Gin
75g caster sugar
Finely grated rind from 1 orange
Finely grated rind from 1 lime

For the pastry

175g plain flour
45ml caster sugar
115g chilled butter diced
Pinch of salt
1 egg yolk

Ginstruction

- Make the pastry by sifting the flour, sugar and salt on to a cold work surface. Make a well in the centre and put in the diced butter and egg yolk. Gradually work the flour into the diced butter and egg yolk, using your finger tips.
- Gather the dough together, reserve about a quarter of the dough for the lattice pattern on the top during decoration. Press the rest into a 23cm fluted tart tin with a removable base. Chill the tin for 30 minutes.
- Meanwhile pre-heat the oven to 190°C and make the filling. Put all the ricotta, cream, eggs, egg yolk, gin, sugar and orange and lemon rinds in a large bowl and beat together until evenly mixed.

- Prick the bottom of the pastry case, then line with foil and fill with baking beans or rice and bake blind for 15 minutes. Then transfer to a wire rack, remove the foil with the beans and allow the tart shell to cool in the tin.
- Spoon the cheese and cream filling into the pastry case and level the surface. Roll out the reserved dough and cut into strips. Arrange the strips on top of the filling in a lattice pattern, sticking them in place with water.
- Bake for 30-35 minutes until golden and set. Transfer to a wire rack and leave to cool, and then carefully remove the side of the tin, leaving the cheesecake on the tin base.

* Serves 6-8

Citrus Fudge

with Citrus Gin

Gingredients

200g cream
100g sugar
15g butter
50ml Citrus Gin
30g candied orange peel
15g ground black pepper

Ginstruction

- Place the butter, whipping cream and sugar, to a saucepan on low heat keep stir until it forms a liquid. Slowly take up the heat and boil to 120°C.
- Be careful not to stir. Take off the heat and wait for it to cool.
- Fold in the orange peel and ground black pepper. Gently fold in the gin 5ml at time and mix until it is combined.
- Continue stirring until its stiff. Grease and line a baking tin with greaseproof paper and grease that. Pour the mixture into the tin. Refrigerate for 6-12 hours until set.

Citrus Slush
with Citrus Gin

Gingredients

480g lychee or apple juice
240ml tonic water
20g gelatine powder
60ml *Ginologist* Citrus Gin
40g chopped oranges segments
40g chopped grapefruit segments
40g chopped apples

Ginstruction

- Sponge the gelatine on 70ml of the juice.
- Mix the remaining juice and tonic water and bring to the boil.
- Melt the gelatine in the microwave and whisk into the juice and tonic water.
- Add the gin and the fruit.
- Pour into a bowl and place in the freezer for 60-90 minutes until it resembles slush.
- Use a fork to break it up and if until liquidly place back in the freezer until it is slushy.
- Pour into large wine glasses and serve.

* Serves 12

Strawberry Spice Turnovers
with Spice Gin

Gingredients

25ml *Ginologist* Spice Gin
1 sheet puff pastry, thawed
64g "Nutella" or similar spread
64g finely chopped strawberries
1 egg, beaten
Handful of raspberries
Powdered sugar

Ginstruction

- Pre-heat oven to 200°C.
- Line a baking tray with baking paper.
- Unfold your thawed puff pastry dough.
- Cut the dough into four equal squares.
- Blend together 10 tablespoons of Nutella, Spice gin and finely chopped strawberries thoroughly in a small bowl.
- Place about 2½ tablespoons of Nutella mixture into the corner of each square of puff pastry.
- Fold the pastry diagonally and crumple the edges together with a fork.
- Brush beaten egg over the folded pastries.
- Bake for 18-20 minutes, or until pastry is golden brown.
- Sprinkle with powdered sugar and raspberries.

* Serves 2-4

Blueberry & Thyme Cheesecake
with **Fl**oral Gin

Gingredients

Biscuit Base

250g digestive biscuits
150g coconut tea biscuits
50g fresh ginger
110g melted (and cooled) butter
50g shredded coconut
10ml *Ginoligist* Floral Gin

Filling

250g cream cheese
250g mascarpone cheese
225ml condensed milk
5 sheets gelatine
50ml *Ginoligist* Floral Gin

Topping

200g blueberries
3 sprigs thyme
25ml Floral Gin
50g caster sugar
100ml water

Ginstruction

- Add the biscuits, ginger, sugar and coconut into a food processor and blitz until it looks like bread crumbs.
- Put into a bowl and add the melted butter and gin, and mix to just combined.
- Press the mixture into the springform pan and all the way up the sides.
- Brush with some melted butter. Bake in the oven at 180°C for 7 minutes.
- Soften the gelatine leaves in cold water.
- Place the cream cheese, mascarpone and condensed milk and gin into a mixing bowl and using the paddle attachment mix until combined.
- Add the gin and gelatine leaves to the above mixture and mix with the whisk attachment.
- Add the thyme sprigs to the gin and leave to infuse for 3-4 days.
- Place the blueberries, 2 springs of thyme, the sugar and water into a bowl and bring to a boil.
- Pour the thyme and gin mixture into the berry coulis and mix.
- Leave to cool.
- Pour the filling into the baked base and place into the fridge overnight to set.
- Top with the topping and serve.

* Serves 4-6

Colombian Mousse Meringue
with Floral Gin

Gingredients

60ml *Ginologist* Floral Gin
2 tsp ground coffee beans
Boiling water
1 tbsp cornflour
100g almond flour
6 egg whites
250g ground icing sugar
125g single cream
75g ground coffee beans
400g milk chocolate (in the region of 50-65 percent cocoa)
4 egg yolks
375ml whipped double/heavy cream.

Ginstruction

- Pre-heat oven to 120°C.
- Place 2 tsp ground coffee in a small bowl, pour over ½ tsp boiling water and stir until the coffee is dissolved. Set aside.
- Mix to combine the cornflour and almond flour and set aside.
- Whisk eggwhites until stiff peaks form. Gradually add the sugar, scrape down the sides of the bowl and beat for a further 2-3 minutes.
- Add the cornflour mixture and coffee and whisk until just combined. Lay down baking/parchment paper on a baking tray.
- Turn a springform tin over and trace two circles using the outside circumference onto the baking paper.

- Divide mixture evenly into both circles and spread so the tops are even.
- Bake for 60-65 minutes or until the meringue is just crisp. Turn the oven off and allow the meringues to cool in the oven with the door closed for 2 hours.
- Lay down baking paper on a baking tray.
- To make the coffee mousse, place the gin, cream and coffee in a heatproof bowl over a saucepan of simmering water and stir until the coffee begins to dissolve.
- Add the chocolate and stir occasionally until the mixture is smooth.
- Allow to cool for 10 minutes. Add the egg yolks and mix thoroughly.
- Place the egg whites in a bowl and whisk until a soft peaks form.
- Fold through the chocolate mixture until combined.
- Add the cream and whisk to combine. Refrigerate for 15 minutes.
- Line the base and sides of a lightly greased springform tin with baking/parchment paper.
- Carefully loosen the meringues from the baking/parchment paper and place 1 meringue in the base of the tin.
- Spoon the mousse into the tin and top with remaining meringue.
- Refrigerate for 3-4 hours or until set.
- Remove once set and lightly dust with icing sugar before serving.

* Serves 4-6

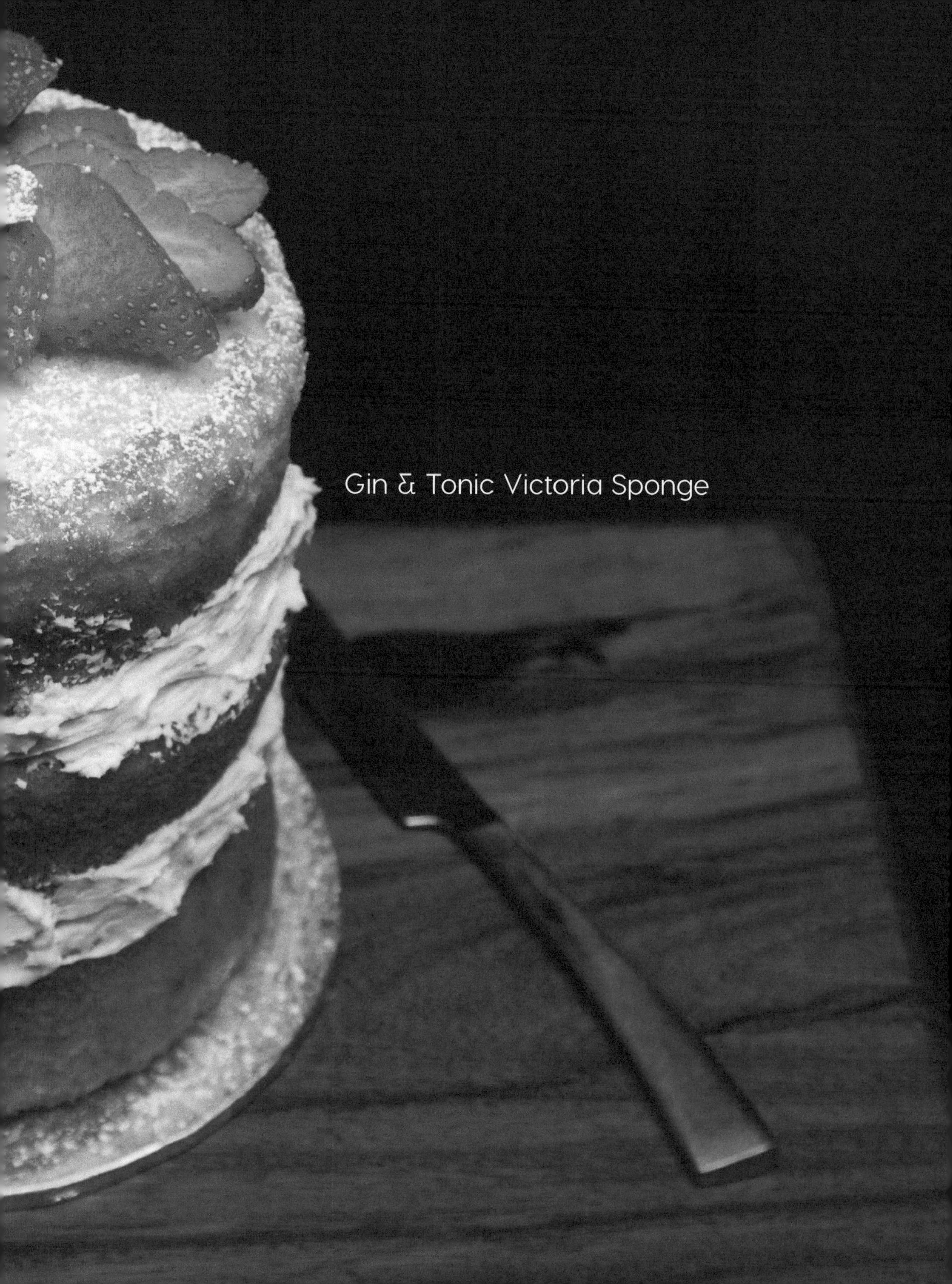

Gin & Tonic Victoria Sponge

Gin & Tonic Victoria Sponge
with Spice Gin

Gingredients

Sponge

250g butter
5ml lemon essence
160g sugar
4 eggs
250g flour
5ml baking powder
15ml *Ginologist* Spice Gin
60ml tonic water

Syrup

50g sugar
100g tonic water
15ml *Ginologist* Spice Gin

Filling

250ml cream
15ml caster sugar
10ml lemon essence

Ginstruction

Sponge

- Cream the butter with the lemon essence.
- Add the sugar and continue to cream.
- Add the eggs one at a time, and continue to beat.
- Combine the gin & tonic.
- Sift the flour and the baking powder together add half the flour mixture and mix until just combines.
- Add the gin & tonic mixture, and mix until combined.
- Add the remaining flour mixture.
- Pour into 2 greased cake pans.
- Bake at 170°C for 30 minutes until golden brown and until a skewer comes out clean.

Gin & Tonic Syrup

- Pour the sugar and tonic water in a saucepan and bring to the boil until the sugar dissolves.
- Take off the stove and add the gin.
- Pour the syrup over the sponges and let sit for 30 minutes.
- In a clean bowl whip the cream, sugar and vanilla essence until stiff peaks form.

To Assemble

- Add the whipped cream to the sponges and stack.
- Dust with icing sugar and serve.

* Serves 6-8

Rose water Crème Brûlée Flamed
with Spice Gin

Gingredients

6 egg yolks
6 tbsp white sugar
½ tsp vanilla extract
625ml heavy cream
60ml Rose syrup or 2 tsp rose water essence.
60ml *Ginologist* Spice Gin

Ginstruction

- Pre-heat oven to 150°C
- Beat egg yolks, 4 tbsp white sugar and vanilla extract along with the Rose syrup/rose water essence in a mixing bowl until thick and creamy.
- Pour cream into a saucepan and stir over low heat until it almost comes to a boil.
- Remove the cream from heat immediately. Stir cream into the egg yolk mixture. Beat until combined.
- Pour cream mixture into the top pan of a double boiler, add the gin. Stir over simmering water until mixture lightly coats the back of a spoon, about 3 minutes. Remove mixture from heat immediately and pour into a shallow heat proof ramekin.
- Bake in pre-heated oven for 30 minutes. Remove from oven and cool to room temperature. Refrigerate for at least 1 hour or overnight.
- In a small bowl combine remaining 2 tbsp white sugar and brown sugar. Sprinkle over the top of custard and torch with a blow torch until sugar has dissolved and caramelized. Serve immediately.

* Serves 4-6

Moroccan Fruit Salad... Gone Wild!

with **Fl**oral Gin

Gingredients

1 red apple, chopped
1 mango, peeled and diced
2 bananas, sliced
2 kiwi fruits, diced
1 orange, diced
64g green grapes
1 large shot (about 45ml *Ginologist* Floral Gin)

Ginstruction

- Place fruits in a bowl, pour gin over fruits, and mix to combine.
- Place fruit and gin mixture in the fridge to infuse for 30 minutes to an hour.
- Remove from fridge, divide, and serve as part of a champagne or hangover breakfast, as a palate cleanser between courses (in a smaller portion), or with ice cream or custard as dessert, or plain as a snack.

* Serves 2

Gin Tart
with Spice Gin

Gingredients

50ml *Ginologist* Spice Gin
200g butter
200g caster sugar
4 medium eggs
200g self-raising flour
1 tsp baking powder
½ tsp mixed spice
zest **½** orange
150ml pear simple syrup
6 tbsp apricot jam
Vanilla
100g mix of dried cranberries, apricots and peaches

Ginstruction

- Soak the dried fruit in the gin and simple syrup for an hour.
- Butter 6 cupcake moulds. Heat oven to 180°C.
- Beat the butter and sugar together thoroughly.
- Beat the eggs, then slowly add them to the butter and sugar while whisking.
- Sift the flour and baking powder together, then spoon into the egg, butter and sugar mixture.
- Drain the fruit and fold into the mix with the mixed spice, orange zest.
- Fill each mould with mixture. Divide jam between each mould.
- Divide remainder of mixture evenly between moulds.
- Bake for about 45-60 minutes or until they have risen and cooked.
- Allow to cool. Chill. Re-heat and gently loosen in to plates with a sharp knife.

* Serves 6

G & T Sorbet

with Spice, Citrus or Floral Gin

Gingredients

25ml *Ginologist* Citrus OR Floral OR Spice Gin
1 can tonic water (200ml)
2 egg whites
Finely grated zest of lemon
2 tbsp icing sugar

Ginstruction

- Whisk egg whites and sugar into a peak.
- Mix Gin, tonic and lemon zest into the mixture.
- Whisk vigorously for a couple of minutes.
- Put into a freezer-safe container and store in the freezer.
- Whisk the mixture every 30 minutes to an hour.
- Repeat this process five times.
- Allow to freeze and enjoy.

* Serves 2-4

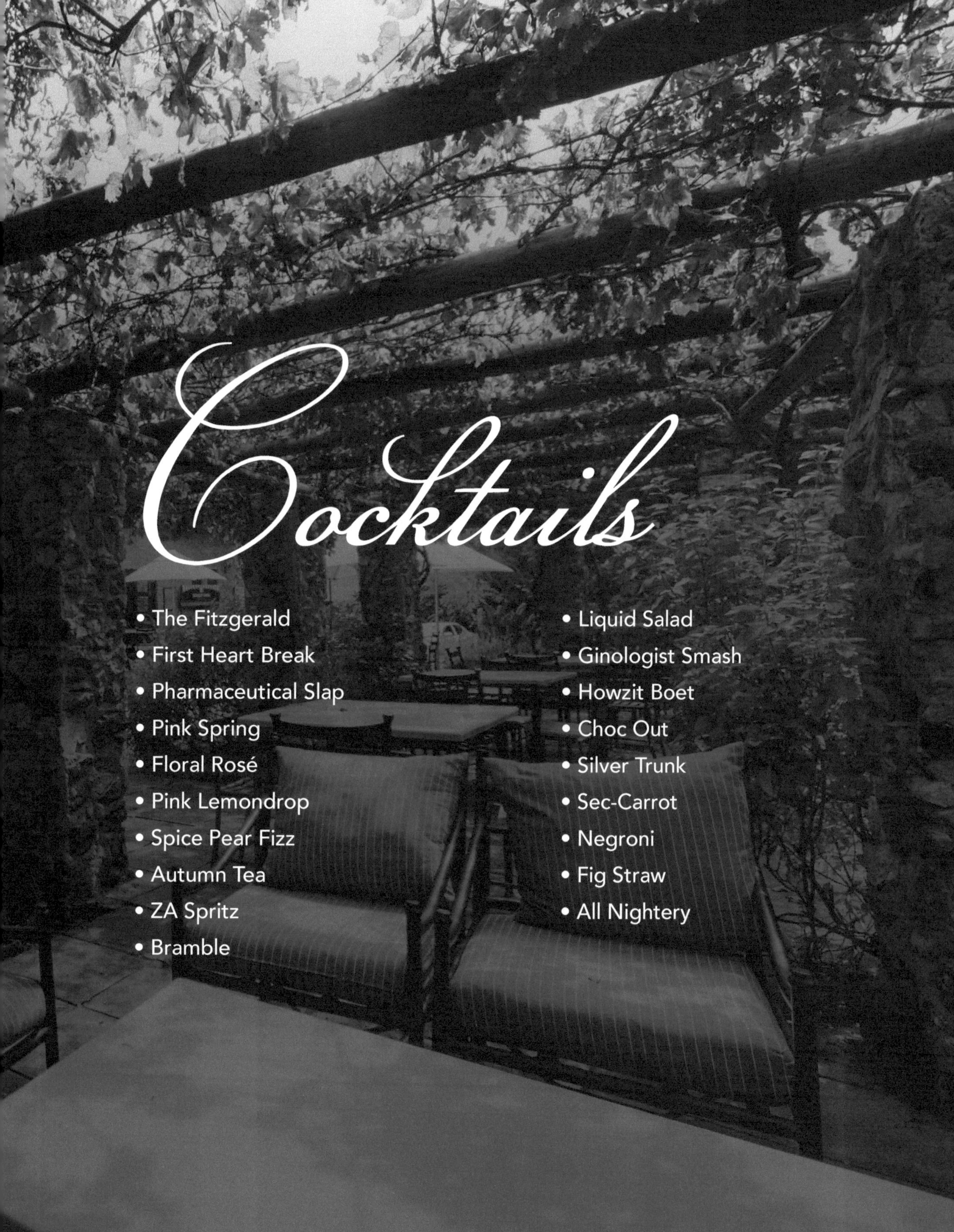

Cocktails

- The Fitzgerald
- First Heart Break
- Pharmaceutical Slap
- Pink Spring
- Floral Rosé
- Pink Lemondrop
- Spice Pear Fizz
- Autumn Tea
- ZA Spritz
- Bramble
- Liquid Salad
- Ginologist Smash
- Howzit Boet
- Choc Out
- Silver Trunk
- Sec-Carrot
- Negroni
- Fig Straw
- All Nightery

The
Mixologist
Ahe Jafta

"A good Gin cocktail makes any occasion a **celebration!**"
GINOLOGIST

The Fitzgerald
with Citrus Gin

Gingredients

50ml *Ginologist* Citrus Gin
Mint simple syrup
Lemon peel ribbon
Angostura bitters
Soda water
Tonic water
1 shaker
Tumbler
Crushed ice

Ginstruction

- Add gin, syrup and bitters to shaker. Shake well for 10 seconds.
- Fill glass with crushed ice. Empty shaker contents into glass.
- Fill tumbler   of the way to the top with tonic water.
- Top off with soda water. Garnish with lemon peel ribbon.

* Serves 1

First Heart Break
with Floral Gin

Gingredients

50ml *Ginologist* Floral Gin
20ml lemon juice
20ml hibiscus syrup
30ml egg white
2 drops of grenadine

Garnish

Dry hibiscus leaves.

Ginstruction

Reverse dry shake (martini glass).

* Serves 1

Pharmaceutical Slap
with Spice Gin

Gingredients

50ml *Ginologist* Spice Gin
20ml coffee liqueur
10ml jäger
10ml sugar syrup
Single espresso fresh

Garnish

Coffee beans

Ginstruction

Shaken (old fashioned or medical cup).
* Serves 1

Pink Spring
with Floral Gin

Gingredients

25ml *Ginologist* Floral Gin
100ml pink lemonade
Rose petals
Tarragon (fresh)
Soda water
Stemless wine glass
Ice cubes

Ginstruction

- Add gin, lemonade and rose petals to glass.
- Fill glass with ice. Stir well.
- Top up with soda water and garnish with tarragon.
- [Optional] Add 15ml simple strawberry syrup before adding soda water.

* Serves 1

Floral Rosé
with **Fl**oral Gin

Gingredients

50ml *Ginologist* Floral Gin
10ml whipping cream
½ egg white
5ml fresh lime juice
5ml fresh lemon juice
10ml simple syrup (unflavoured)
2 dashes orange bitters (roughly **¼** tsp)
Sparkling rosé to top
Slice of lemon (dried) to garnish
1 shaker
1 julep strainer
Ice cubes

Ginstruction

- Add all *gingredients* the egg white, lemon slice and sparkling rosé added into a shaker with cubed ice.
- Shake vigorously for 25 seconds.
- Remove ice with strainer.
- Add egg white.
- Shake vigorously for 25 seconds.
- Pour into chilled martini glass.
- Pour sparkling rosé gently into glass.
- Garnish with lemon slice.

* Serves 1

Pink Lemondrop
with Citrus Gin OR Floral Gin

Gingredients

25ml *Ginologist* Citrus Gin OR *Ginologist* Floral Gin
25ml raspberry simple syrup
60ml lemon juice
37½ml Cointreau or similar orange-flavoured liqueur
15ml whipping cream
1 shaker
1 martini glass
Ice cubes
Hawthorne strainer

Ginstruction

- Add all ingredients to shaker.
- Shake vigorously for 1 minute.
- Add ice cubes to shaker.
- Shake vigorously for 15 seconds.
- Strain into martini glass using hawthorne strainer.
- Garnish with remaining raspberries.

* Serves 1

Spice Pear Fizz
with Spice Gin

Gingredients

1 pear
2 whole star anise
1 egg white (or glucose syrup)
10ml freshly squeezed lemon juice
1 can of club soda
128g sugar
250ml water
30ml *Ginologist* Spice Gin
1 shaker
1 Hawthorne strainer
And ice cubes

Ginstruction

- Simple pear syrup.
- Dice pear.
- Add to pan sugar and water.
- Heat until sugar dissolves.
- Add pear dices.
- Allow to cool.
- Remove pear dices and keep cold .

Cocktail

- Add egg white, 30ml Ginologist Spice, club soda, 20ml simple syrup and 10ml lemon juice to shaker
- Shake vigorously for 1 minute
- Add cubed ice to shaker
- Shake vigorously for 30 seconds
- Strain contents through Hawthorne strainer into champagne coupe
- Garnish with whole star anise Autumn type

* Serves 1

Autumn Tea
with **Fl**oral Gin

Gingredients

37½ml *Ginologist* Floral Gin
Sprig of rosemary
Edible flowers
Chamomile simple syrup
Orange juice
50ml prosecco
Champagne flute

Ginstruction

- Add gin, simple syrup and prosecco to flute (stir well).
- Top off with orange juice.
- Garnish with edible flowers and rosemary.

* Serves 1

ZA Spritz
with Floral Gin

Gingredients

50ml *Ginologist* Floral Gin
30ml aperol
20ml rooibos syrup
Sparkling dry rosé

Garnish

Orange wheel

Ginstruction

Build (served in a burgundy glass).
* Serves 1

Bramble
with Citrus Gin

Gingredients

50ml *Ginologist* Citrus Gin
4 blackberriers
20ml sugar
20ml lime
Crème de mûre (blackberry liqueur) float

Garnish

Fresh blackberries

Ginstruction

Shaken (old fashioned).
* Serves 1

Liquid Salad
with Floral Gin

Gingredients

50ml *Ginologist* Floral Gin
15ml lime
15ml agave
10ml cucumber juice
10ml fresh apple juice

Garnish

Cucumber slice

Ginstruction

Shaken (old fashioned glass).
* Serves 1

Ginologist Smash
with Citrus Gin

Gingredients

50ml *Ginologist* Citrus Gin
Half a peach
30ml lemon
15ml sugar syrup
30ml triple sec
6 fresh mint leaves

Garnish

Mint sprig and peach slice

Ginstruction

Muddle shaken (served in an old-fashioned glass).
* Serves 1

Howzit Boet

*an authentic South African cocktail

with Floral Gin

Gingredients

50ml *Ginologist* Floral Gin
20ml *peppermint liqueur*
10ml cream
10ml amarula (cream) lique
5ml spice syrup

Garnish

Mint leaf

Ginstruction

Shaken
(served in a martini glass).

* Serves 1

Choc Out
with Spice Gin

Gingredients

50ml *Ginologist* Spice Gin
20ml chocolate liqueur
10ml lime juice
10ml cinnamon syrup
2 dash chocolate bitters
Milk stout top-up

Garnish

Flamed cinnamon bark + dark chocolate flakes

Ginstruction

Shaken (brandy balloon).
* Serves 1

Silver Trunk
with Citrus Gin

Gingredients

50ml *Ginologist* Citrus Gin
5ml extra dry vermouth
5ml sweet vermouth
5ml amarula
30ml egg white
30ml fresh pineapple juice

Garnish

Cocktail cherry

Ginstruction

Reverse dry shake (martini glass).
* Serves 1

Sec-Carrot
with Spice Gin

Gingredients

50ml *Ginologist* Spice Gin
25ml triple sec
30ml carrot juice
30ml grapefruit juice
3 carrot leaves
3 parsley leaves

Garnish

Carrot leaves and parsley

Ginstruction

Bruise and shaken (old fashioned glass).

* Serves 1

Negroni
with Citrus Gin

Gingredients

20ml *Ginologist* Citrus Gin
20ml Campari (or similar)
20ml sweet vermouth
20ml fresh tangerine juice
Orange foam

Garnish

Orange foam and candied orange peel

Ginstruction

Stirred (old fashioned).

* Serves 1

Fig Straw
with Citrus Gin

Gingredeints

50ml *Ginologist* Citrus Gin
20ml lime juice
2 tsp fig jam
2 tsp strawberry jam
20ml apricot brandy
Lemonade top-up

Garnish

Dry figs

Ginstruction:

Shaken (old fashioned crushed ice).

* Serves 1

All Nightery
with Spice Gin

Gingredients

50ml *Ginologist* Spice Gin
30ml fresh beetroot juice
30ml spinach juice
20ml lemon
20ml honey water
10ml triple sec

Garnish

Slice of beetroot and a baby spinach leaf

Ginstruction

Shaken (high ball glass).

* Serves 1

Published by:

GBP Publishing Org
619 Wey House
15 Church Street
Weybridge
Surrey
KT13 8NA
United Kingdom

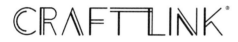

FOX STREET JHB
CRAFTLINK®
DISTILLERY

Craft Link Distillery
1 Fox Street
1Fox Precinct
Johannesburg
South Africa

The Ginologist Cook Book was photographed at Hemingways Restaurant at Leriba Hotel, Centurian, South Africa

Best Restaurant in SA at the Welcome Awards 2011
Best Fine Dining Restaurant in SA, 2011 and 2012

Index

CITRUS GIN

COCONUT

CRÈME BRÛLÉE

CURRY

DUCK

FISH

FLORAL GIN

FUDGE

LAMB

SORBET

SOUP

SPICE GIN

Spiced Sweet Potato 49
Spicy Fruit Cake from Siena 213
Strawberry Spice Turnovers 229
Summer Prawn Spring Rolls 80
Teriyaki Salmon 138 138
Thai Spice Chicken Burger 142
The Day After Cheat Day Cookies 216
The Manly Man 88
Tomato Chutney 148

SPRING ROLLS

Summer Prawn Spring Rolls 80
Vegetable Spring Rolls in Rice Paper 56

STRAWBERRY

Eton Mess 220
Lime & Ginger Panna cotta with Boiled Black Peppers, Strawberry & Ginologist Floral Compote, served with Matcha Tuile Biscuit 178
Strawberry Spice Turnovers 229